THINKING COLLABORATIVELY

Thinking Collaboratively is a theoretical and practical guide to thinking and learning in deep and meaningful ways within purposeful communities of inquiry. Critical thinking has long been recognized as an important educational goal but, until now, has largely been conceived and operationalized as an individual attitude and ability. Increasingly, however, a more relevant and complete cognitive construct has been emerging: *thinking collaboratively*. Thinking collaboratively is the means to inquire, test, and apply new understandings, and to make sense of the information that bombards us continuously. In short, thinking collaboratively is required to flourish in our highly connected world and, in this book based on more than a decade of research, Garrison provides an essential introduction to this vital concept.

D. Randy Garrison is a retired professor of the Werklund School of Education at the University of Calgary, Canada. Dr Garrison has published extensively on teaching and learning in adult, higher, and distance education contexts. He has authored, co-authored, or edited 11 books and well over 100 refereed articles and chapters. He has also won several awards including the 2009 Sloan Consortium Award for Most Outstanding Achievement in Online Learning by an Individual.

THINKING COLLABORATIVELY

Learning in a Community of Inquiry

D. Randy Garrison

Routledge
Taylor & Francis Group

NEW YORK AND LONDON

First published 2016
by Routledge
711 Third Avenue, New York, NY 10017

and by Routledge
2 Park Square, Milton Park, Abingdon, Oxon OX14 4RN

Routledge is an imprint of the Taylor & Francis Group, an informa business

© 2016 Taylor & Francis

Library of Congress Cataloging in Publication Data
A catalog record for this book has been requested.

ISBN: 978-1-138-82431-7 (hbk)
ISBN: 978-1-138-82432-4 (pbk)
ISBN: 978-1-315-74075-1 (ebk)

Typeset in Bembo
by Cenveo Publisher Services

CONTENTS

PREFACE

The genesis of this book is the insights that emerged from more than a decade of collaborative research on thinking and learning in a community of inquiry. The focus of this research was on the transactional dynamics of learning through collaborative inquiry – an approach that is both a catalyst and facilitator for deep and meaningful learning. Thinking and learning in collaborative settings provide an environment where participants engage in critical reflection and discourse. The intended outcomes are not only personal meaning but mutual understanding. Thinking and learning collaboratively is a process of engaging with new ideas, raising questions, and clarifying misunderstandings.

Man has never been a solitary thinker nor predisposed to critically examining personal perspectives and beliefs. We are social beings interacting with our challenging and complex surroundings. In fact our very evolution is linked to collaboration (Wilson 2012). Perhaps it is time that in a connected knowledge society we explicitly recognize and understand the importance of collaboration in our thinking and learning. The argument is that thinking collaboratively is a transactional learning experience and an essential process for overcoming personal bias (tendency to hold to current beliefs and reject new ideas). Moreover, thinking collaboratively is inevitably associated with critical and creative thought processes that lead to deep and meaningful learning experiences. Consistent with this perspective, the construct of thinking and learning collaboratively is described and developed within the Community of Inquiry framework. It is this framework that provides the theoretical coherence to understand and apply collaborative thinking and learning in socially situated and technologically connected learning environments.

The work on the Community of Inquiry framework began in the late 1990s with collaboration among myself, Terry Anderson, and Walter Archer (see Garrison, Anderson and Archer 2010). During the early stages of this research we had created a small community of inquiry without thinking of it in such terms. While being friends and colleagues helped immeasurably in terms of trust and communication, the unique element of our success was the different set of interests, knowledge and experiences that we were able to blend together to resolve a challenge we were facing in the delivery of online courses in a blended graduate program. At the time there was little research and virtually no coherent perspective in which to help us understand online learning. In relatively short order, however, we constructed what has become a widely adopted, credible and robust theoretical framework for the study and design of online and blended learning. The reasons for its success are many but at its core is a parsimonious and intuitive conceptualization of a complex dynamic.

The Community of Inquiry framework was the result of a constructive process of thinking collaboratively. We were thinking collaboratively as we tried to understand and describe the process of thinking and learning in a virtual world. The collaborative nature of this research continued as the research community expanded and the framework developed theoretically and practically. The success of this research was a direct result of sustained and focused collaborative thinking and learning, very much as described by the Community of Inquiry framework. We were modeling the very process that we were trying to describe.

From a personal perspective, this book reflects the culmination of a career exploring thinking and learning in a variety of contexts that included higher, adult and distance education. My first academic position was as a director of distance education in a traditional university context. Not having much experience in the field, I had trouble accepting that the goal of distance education at the time was to write course packages that would make the learner as independent as possible (described in Chapter 4). To me this seemed to contradict the very nature of an educational experience. Education in the traditional literature is grounded in two-way communication. My earliest writing at the time (Garrison 1989) attempted to address this theme and has shaped my research since.

Other early areas of study that caught my attention were critical thinking and self-directed learning. The critical thinking research (Garrison 1991) evolved into the Practical Inquiry model and a core element of the

Community of Inquiry framework. The Practical Inquiry model reflected the reality and fusion of reflection and discourse and is central to the concept of thinking and learning collaboratively described here. The work on self-directed learning (Garrison 1997a) became a jumping off point for our recent work on shared metacognition as manifested in a community of inquiry. Shared metacognition is essential for thinking and learning collaboratively and brings me full circle back to my early interest in how we think. Shared metacognition is a comprehensive understanding of thinking and learning that explicitly recognizes social influences and the importance of collaboration.

The point is that the most satisfying and well received work that I have done has invariably been the result of extensive collaboration with my colleagues and graduate students over the years (I will not attempt to provide a list because it is long and lest I forget somebody). However, I would be remiss if I did not acknowledge three of my colleagues (Norm Vaughan, Marti Cleveland-Innes and Zehra Akyol) who have sustained me beyond my date of expected retirement. My collaborations over the years have brought together a range of expertise, generated a synergy of ideas and a motivational state hard to maintain as an individual. The collaborations stimulated and sustained my interest and continued involvement in exploring and interpreting particular aspects of the framework. The Community of Inquiry framework, research methodology and principles of practice was not and could not have been the work of one person. It is a testament to thinking and learning collaboratively.

Contents

The first chapter provides the context and argument for the consideration of thinking and learning collaboratively. The chapter explores societal developments pointing to the necessities for thinking and learning collaboratively. Chapter 2 provides an historical perspective for thinking and learning collaboratively. The chapter begins with the work of Dewey, Vygotsky and Piaget and then moves to more recent work on cognition. Chapter 3 explores how technology is both a disruptive and constructively transformative force. The chapter describes how technology can support an environment for deep learning by sustaining connections and creating opportunities for thinking and learning collaboratively. It is shown how technology can provide the opportunity to think collaboratively and build learning communities that remain connected over time and place. The fourth chapter provides an historical context to the educational developments that have led us to the era of engagement. The chapter concludes the first part of the book that provides the foundational ideas and developments that have led to a focus on thinking and learning collaboratively.

The fifth chapter moves us into a specific discussion of what it means to think collaboratively and the practical considerations for creating learning experiences that can capitalize on this approach. Chapter 5 sets the stage for subsequent discussions by describing the Community of Inquiry framework. This framework provides the constructs to understand the dynamic of thinking and learning collaboratively. Particular attention is given to thinking and learning collaboratively as the interdependence between cognitive and teaching presence in an environment that provides the social presence to support collaborative inquiry. Chapter 6 documents recent research with regard to the theoretical coherence of the framework and developments in understanding the presences. This provides a more detailed understanding of the dynamics of a community of inquiry. The seventh chapter explores the practical implications of the Community of Inquiry through seven derived principles. This chapter describes the principles and explores the practical implications for thinking and learning collaboratively. Chapter 8 explores the resistance of higher education to thinking and learning collaboratively through the lens of leadership. It is argued that at the organizational level collaborative leadership is essential to shift from individual to collaborative thinking in order to initiate and sustain strategic action. The final chapter summarizes the central themes for thinking and learning collaboratively.

In summary, the construct of thinking and learning collaboratively is grounded in research on critical and reflective thinking but is more comprehensively defined within the Community of Inquiry framework. It is hoped that the contribution of this book will add to understanding thinking and learning in purposeful learning communities that can be sustained over time and space. My final comment and wish is for the reader to have the opportunity to engage in thinking collaboratively about the contents of this book. That is, to engage in reflective discourse, to practice thinking collaboratively, while reading about the very topic.

D. R. Garrison
2015

1

INTRODUCTION

It does not seem possible to account for the cognitive accomplishments of our species by reference to what is inside our heads alone.

(Hutchins 2000)

Thinking is not a private experience. This seemingly paradoxical statement suggests that thinking somehow extends beyond individual rationality and creativity. The reality is that much of human evolution is socially situated and dependent upon collaboration (Wilson 2012). So the question is, why should this be any different when it comes to perhaps the most distinctive human characteristic – thinking? The fact is that thinking has always been socially situated and thinking collaboratively is an innately human characteristic. Thinking is deeply embedded in our environment and the shared experiences of those with whom we engage. However, this is becoming more apparent and relevant in the context of a shrinking technological world. The enhanced opportunities for engagement in a technologically connected society raise important questions about the role the environment plays in stimulating and shaping thinking and learning.

The creative and innovative benefits of thinking collaboratively have been known for some time. Historically, the success of thinking collaboratively has been evident in the medical and biological fields distinguished by collaborative approaches to research and development. One of the best historical examples is the integrated group practice of the Mayo Clinic that pioneered team work and collaboration in pooling the disparate expertise of various disciplines. This produced a level of excellence simply not possible in a traditional doctor's office. Other well-known historical examples are Thomas Edison's Menlo Park laboratory and those of Bell and IBM labs. The groundbreaking story of the discovery of the double helix by Watson, Crick and Wilkins was another well-known example of team-based research.

Perhaps the best known current examples are the collaborative approaches clearly evident in the outstandingly successful information and communication technology companies such as Google and Facebook. The collaborative nature of the digital revolution is described very well by Isaacson (2014). He notes that the computer and Internet inventions were not conjured up by individual geniuses. The lone inventor is largely a myth. Isaacson (2014) has described how inventors and entrepreneurs "collaborated and why their ability to work as teams made them even *more* creative" (p. 1). This is why deep and meaningful learning is a team endeavor – a process of thinking and learning collaboratively. Shared thinking help us to make sense of experiences while opening our own thoughts and beliefs to examination and testing. The purpose here is to explore more deeply this collaborative process of creative and critical thinking.

Thinking collaboratively is an essential component of innovative thinking and learning. Thinking collaboratively is about developing critical thinking, communication and problem-solving skills. It creates an environment for synergistic ideation and innovation. The challenge is how to structure environments for innovative thinking and learning. A core reason for encouraging shared thinking and learning is that humans are inherently selective in seeing and reinforcing existing beliefs. If thinking is to be innovative, there is a need to break out of this cognitive straightjacket and to consider new ideas; to overcome the human bias to confirm and not question currently held perspectives and ideas. Experience and evidence is unwittingly selected and interpreted to fit within the individual's personal paradigm. This reluctance to explore conflicting arguments or ideas is well known in science (Kuhn 1962). If this is the case with those committed to the rigor of the scientific method, then there is clearly a need to address the predisposition to confirm our personal biases in educational contexts. We all have blind spots that need to be recognized. Constructing personal meaning without critical feedback can be inherently satisfying but it can also be delusional. This is the core argument and rationale for the adoption of collaborative approaches to thinking and learning operationalized during the inquiry process.

The perspective I offer here is that thinking collaboratively is a form of inquiry engaged in by a purposeful and supportive community of learners that can be enhanced and sustained through communication technologies. Thinking collaboratively is dependent upon constructing a culture of inquiry in the context of purposeful, engaged, and trusting communities. The broader justification for thinking collaboratively is revealed in the finding that companies are far more successful when built on a culture of collaboration (Rohman 2014a). It must be realized that: "Nowadays, though we may still idolize the charismatic leader or creative genius, almost every decision of consequence is made by a group" (Woolley *et al.* 2015, 2nd paragraph). Innovation in thinking and learning is intimately associated with the practice of thinking collaboratively in a culture of inquiry – where learners can collaboratively explore, construct, test and apply knowledge. In a technologically connected world where so much information is literally at our fingertips, we must understand the conditions for thinking critically and collaboratively if we are to address the complex problems we face in an increasingly connected society and knowledge economy.

Foundational Constructs

The philosophical foundation for exploring thinking collaboratively is pro-vided by John Dewey and his rejection of dualistic approaches (self and other) to thinking and learning. The rejection of dualistic thinking raises a dilemma for the thesis explored here. On the surface, one might consider the phrase "thinking collaboratively" an oxymoron. How can a latent, intel-lectual process extend beyond the mind of the individual and be a collabo-rative process? If it is so, what is the nature of this relationship between the internal private and external shared world?

Exploring the concept that thinking is both a personal reflective and shared process is the journey we take in this book. It is a rejection of the separation between personal and shared worlds in the process of thinking and learning. Individuals are social beings and thinking and learning is a social endeavor. One simply does not exist without the other. Only in the abstract can we imagine the individual thinking in isolation. Few would argue that we are not nourished intellectually and emotionally through the interactions with others and their ideas. Moreover, it is becoming increas-ingly apparent that the individual cannot succeed in the increasingly inter-connected and interdependent world without think collaboratively.

Thinking collaboratively is personal reflection fused with critical dis-course where ideas can be challenged. The basic challenge and goal in a connected society is being able to make sense of the information that continuously bombards us. Access or proximity to information and knowledge is intimately associated with innovative thinking. Thinking collaboratively is the transactional means to inquire, test new information, and apply new ideas. Thinking collaboratively is a deep and meaningful approach to learning that relies on critical and creative thinking through sustained engagement with content and other learners. This collaborative approach to thinking extends beyond acquiring information or developing basic competencies. It necessitates that learners assume responsibility and understand intellectual inquiry as constructing personal meaning and confirming understanding through purposeful engagement.

Essential to this process is the validation of personal meaning. At the heart of thinking collaboratively is the reality that we are not very good at diagnosing our individual misconceptions, perceptual biases and faulty logic. We need open and purposeful discourse where ideas can be shared and critically analyzed such that they are subjected to needed checks and balances to correct misconceptions and achieve shared understanding. This knowledge-building way of thinking has become a practical necessity because of recent advancements in ubiquitous information and communication technologies, and in the explosion of information sources. Collaborative thinking is a search for what could and should be the experience of thinking and learning in a connected and knowledge society. In short, thinking collaboratively is a requirement to flourish in an unpredictable connected world that demands innovative thinking and learning and a process that encourages the critical analysis of personal beliefs and meaning.

When we talk about thinking collaboratively we are not talking about a form of collective intelligence or thinking. There is no such entity as collective intelligence. The process of thinking collaboratively can result in collective or public knowledge, but the intelligence behind this dynamic is individuals engaged in reflective discourse with the goal to construct personal meaning but collaboratively confirm understanding. Moreover, collective thinking is a form of non-thinking; of mindlessly following the group and unwilling to reshape one's own thoughts or to challenge the thinking of others. Thinking collaboratively is the opposite of collective thinking (or group-think) in that the goal is the individual exploring and making sense of conflicting ideas or complex situations through discourse and debate. Thinking collaboratively is suited to challenging basic assumptions and solving complex problems. Thinking collaboratively is for the individual to be challenged and to challenge others' perspectives and ideas through collaborative inquiry. The premise here is that thinking collaboratively greatly enhances the construction of personal meaning and shared understanding through disciplined inquiry and continuous critical assessment. Thinking collaboratively demands the individual justify his or her thinking to gain a deep and shared understanding that can contribute to societal knowledge. Thinking collaboratively is a process of situated cognition and not some alien form of collective intelligence.

Technology

Thinking collaboratively is essential in a knowledge-based society that is increasingly supported by a range of information and communication technologies. Creating and sustaining an environment for thinking collaboratively is complex and challenging and is often dependent upon technology. At its core, deep and meaningful approaches to thinking and learning are best assured in connected and collaborative learning environments that exhibit shared interests and purposeful leadership. In this regard, thinking collaboratively is supported and extended through communication technologies. As a result, we need to understand how the connected world is impacting thinking and learning.

It is safe to say that educators have not fully come to grips with understanding the impact of an unpredictable and connected world on thinking and learning. While social media is commonplace, we are still in the early exploratory stage of understanding how this impacts thinking and how we can design worthwhile learning experiences in our technologically connected world. The Internet can help us access information and communicate with others but this must be complemented by the corrective transaction of questioning the validity of the information and collaboratively focusing on worthwhile learning goals. Thinking collaboratively must be centered on purposeful and corrective discourse. Our thoughts are shaped through the connections with others – increasingly through communication technologies. This fusion of people and technology will increasingly provide the means for thinking collaboratively. What is not in question is the need to think collaboratively to construct shared understanding in an increasingly connected society.

To reiterate, we live and learn in socially situated environments that are influenced and shaped by interactions with others. However, communication technologies have expanded and enhanced the collaborative thinking and learning environment through virtual synchronous and asynchronous interactions. Communication technologies create new and sustained opportunities for learners to share their thinking. At the same time, the focus must be on using technology as a tool to inspire and engage learners in a climate of critical inquiry. To paraphrase Henry David Thoreau, technology must be the means to an improved end, not the end itself. Technology must be appropriately applied to create worthwhile learning transactions. Increasingly a community of learners is being perceived as the best means to share our thinking for the purposes of collaboratively constructing meaning and understanding. Technology is introduced to bring learners together to engage in thinking collaboratively in and beyond the classroom.

Communication technologies are not only helping us connect, but they also add to the complexity in our lives and the increased need to think collaboratively. That is, the emergence of communication technologies across society is both a catalyst for the need as well as the means to think collaboratively. The self-reinforcing nature of communication technologies presents a relentless and inescapable reality that is transforming, for better or worse, how we think and learn. Access to and transmission of information is no longer the primary responsibility of educators. Information and communications technology have flattened the educational hierarchy and shifted the emphasis and expertise to issues of participant leadership in thinking and learning collaboratively.

While thinking collaboratively is becoming an imperative with the advancements of communication technologies, it is clear that it is the design, facilitation and direction of reflection and discourse that will have a lasting qualitative impact. It is the leadership and not the technology that makes the qualitative difference in thinking and learning collaboratively. When learners learn with and through technology, it opens enormous possibilities for thinking and learning; however, its true advantage is in supporting communities of learners and the conditions for thinking collaboratively across time and space.

Critical Thinking

Critical thinking was the watchword in educational circles in previous decades. Critical thinking was associated with encouraging a skeptical attitude along with developing individual reflective skills such as logical reasoning and personal judgment. At the same time arose the debate on whether critical thinking was a general ability that could be taught as a distinct subject or whether critical thinking needed to be developed during the process of understanding a specific discipline or body of knowledge. The position that critical thinking must be developed within the context of learning subject matter was put forward by John McPeck (1990). He advanced a pedagogic position that thinking must be honest argument about a particular idea or topic within a specific discipline. It could not be developed in a vacuum. This is clearly our position here. Critical thinking is best learned through the process of learning the nuances of a specific discipline, but thinking is also best developed collaboratively in the environment of the particular discipline.

If the educational experience is not to be confined to assimilating course content, it is important to recognize that a worthwhile learning experience is a transaction that deepens and extends our understanding of the initially inert content. The greatest influence on the direction and quality of thinking is the recognition of these social and collaborative realities associated with intellectual inquiry. We now more fully recognize and appreciate that critical thinking extends beyond the individual and the subject matter – it also includes those to whom we communicate as we construct personal meaning and shared understanding. That is, thinking collaboratively is more than simply sharing information. Thinking collaboratively is about open communication, questioning and problem-solving through inquiry and, ultimately, continuous learning.

The skills of communication and problem-solving have become increasingly important in higher education. It has been stated that:

> Education today is much more about ways of thinking that involve creative and critical approaches to problem-solving and decision-making. It is also about ways of working, including communication and collaboration, as well as the tools they require, such as the capacity to recognise and exploit the potential of new technologies ....
>
> *(Schleicher 2010, p. 2.)*

Consistent with this, a recent survey of employers found that "job candidates are lacking most in written and oral communication skills, adaptability and managing multiple priorities, and making decisions and problem solving" (*The Chronicle of Higher Education* 2012, p.12). These abilities can only be developed in a learning environment that values and supports collaborative inquiry, requiring critical thinking and discourse in resolving dilemmas and solving practical problems. Thinking and learning collaboratively is an imperative in the classroom and workplace.

Innovative and creative thinking is greatly enhanced with the collaboration of others (Hemlin *et al.* 2004; Paulus *et al.* 2003). Thinking collaboratively is a complex dynamic that does not occur in a disciplinary vacuum or in social isolation. The core dynamic in thinking collaboratively is the fusion of reflection and discourse in a purposeful and trusting environment. The goal is more than acquiring information or having an emotionally satisfying experience. Recognizing the collaborative nature of thinking, however, is disruptive to traditional educational systems that are focused on acquiring disciplinary information. With the ubiquitous presence of the Internet and new and emerging communication technologies, information acquisition is no longer the primary challenge. The focus is shifting to leading collaboratively the construction of knowledge. That is, the modern focus is increasingly on the process of thinking and learning in a connected world; a world where insight and innovation is no longer seen as a solitary venture. New and emerging communication technologies are pushing educators to understand and create environments where critical thinking can be nurtured.

The Community of Inquiry

I contend that the ability to think collaboratively is best developed in learning communities that exhibit the conditions of open communication and cohesion (group identity). This goes beyond simply being continuously connected. The challenge is to create an environment that supports the focused synergy of minds through communication and commitment to a common interest and purpose. This is an environment where participants come together to explore an idea or resolve a dilemma, feel free to express their ideas, provide mutual support and constructive feedback. Such an environment describes a community of learners whose purpose is to critically inquire into areas of common interest. Understanding the optimal conditions for thinking collaboratively is to understand the nature of a community of inquiry. The environment for thinking collaboratively goes beyond simple participation and interaction.

Accepting the premise that education is a social and collaborative enterprise, the challenge is to understand the nature and dynamics of thinking collaboratively in a learning community. Many educational theorists, including pioneers such as Dewey and Vygotsky, have argued for collaborative approaches to realize a worthwhile educational experience (Lee and Smagorinsky 2000). Dewey (1933) focused on inquiry as the social process of solving problems and resolving dilemmas. His form of practical inquiry, based on a generalized version of the scientific method, was inherently collaborative. In this regard, it has been stated that the only fully appropriate pedagogy for thinking in education is a community of inquiry approach (Lipman 2003). Engagement with the subject matter and others through fair-minded inquiry provides the best assurance of higher order thinking and learning.

The Community of Inquiry framework describes an environment where participants collaboratively construct meaning and share understanding (Garrison 2011). The Community of Inquiry framework provides a comprehensive and coherent perspective of inquiry where learning is dependent upon the transactional dynamics of the community. Through the interdependent core elements of cognitive, social and teaching presence the Community of Inquiry framework describes the dynamic context for thinking and learning collaboratively. The Community of Inquiry framework provides a coherent, heuristic and proven theoretical framework for studying and designing a community of thinkers and learners. Fifteen years of research has shown us that thinking and learning collaboratively must concurrently consider the interdependence of the core presences as well as the influential support of exogenous variables such as media and communications technology. This framework will be more fully explored in Chapter 5.

Summary

The premise of this book is the reality that individuals think and learn in context. Thinking collaboratively is the dialectic push and pull of the personal, interpretive realities of both the internal and shared worlds of the individual learner. That is, collaboratively reflecting upon ideas and experiences while making reasonable judgments of the validity of personal meaning through critical discourse. The reality of knowledge is the integration of these internal and external perspectives grounded in the rationality of thinking collaboratively. From this perspective there is no such thing as thinking by groups, only thinking in groups. Thinking collaboratively does not diminish individual responsibility to construct meaning and confirm understanding. To help us appreciate the place for thinking collaboratively in an increasingly connected and complex world, we move next to an historical perspective on thinking and learning.

2

THINKING AND LEARNING

The collaboration that created the digital age was not just among peers but also between generations.

(Isaacson 2014, p. 4.)

The idea that great thinkers and artists were solitary geniuses is a myth. This was made evident when Isaac Newton stated: "If I have seen further it is by standing on the shoulders of giants." It is clear that the greatest scientist of all time recognized that none of us think or learn in isolation. The gifted are cultivated in a heritage of knowledge and the influence of contemporaries. The challenge we all face today is the complexity of being able to assess information for its relevance and our sustained interactions with others as we construct personal meaning and confirm mutual understanding.

The amount of information that we have to process in a knowledge society imposes enormous challenges for individuals. Making sense of an avalanche of information and images requires reasoned judgment and critical thinking. Critical thinking is more than self-reflection and is invariably socially situated. It is a form of disciplined inquiry that moves the individual beyond autonomous thought. Personal meaning must be put to the test. We all can too easily succumb to our personal biases and selectively look for evidence to confirm existing and often flawed perspectives and beliefs. It is through sharing our ideas that we are able to assess personal meaning and confirm shared understanding. Only through the process of diagnosing misconceptions and considering alternative conceptions are we able to achieve confidence in our thinking.

The focus here is to understand how thinking can be distributed across a group. What are the conditions for critical thinking and disciplined inquiry in a community of learners? How do leaners collaborate in a way that facilitates critical reflection and discourse? To be sure this is more than sharing information or a set of agreed-upon facts. Thinking collaboratively is a process of critical discourse that includes debate and negotiation of understanding. Our interest here is on the cognitive properties of the individual immersed in the interactions of a group with common academic purposes and interests. Conversely, however, the focus is equally on the dynamics of the group that can enhance the thinking of the individual through purposeful collaborative inquiry. A learning community is concerned with both the cognitive dynamics of the individual AND how the group can stimulate and challenge the thinking of the individual. Each transaction is inseparable and essential in the process of thinking and learning collaboratively.

This inseparability can be demonstrated in an analogy to the functioning of the brain. Thinking in isolation is like thinking with half your brain. While this may sound flippant, the reality is that the brain works best when the focused, logical left side and the scope of the intuitive right side are fully integrated. The power is in the synergy of the rational and the intuitive. So too must the individual be fully integrated with a community of learners that has the potential to integrate the intuitive sense of the individual with the corrective logic of the group. While this analogy is certainly overstated, it does emphasize the essential complementary nature of thinking collaboratively. Collaborative thinking is a whole body experience; that is, an individual is fully engaged, cognitively and transactionally, in a purposeful group of learners.

The premise here is that thinking collaboratively is a socially shared dynamic. The goal and challenge in this chapter is to understand the simultaneously private and shared processes of thinking and learning collaboratively. To understand this dynamic we need to appreciate several areas of research associated with the thinking process and the context in which it occurs. We begin with the considerable body of research commonly classified as critical or reflective thinking.

Critical and Reflective Thinking

Critical thinking has been recognized as an important learning dynamic but is largely conceived and operationalized as an individual attitude and ability. This perspective was reflected in the early research on self-efficacy, self-regulation, personal motivation and metacognition. Increasingly, however, in the connected and collaborative world that exists today, a more relevant and complete cognitive construct is emerging – thinking collaboratively. A construct that moves beyond the self and considers a process of distributed cognition.

It has been argued that critical thinking is an essential ability to prosper in a dynamic knowledge society driven by innovation and change. Considering this perspective, it is not surprising that developing critical thinkers is seen as an explicit goal of higher education. However, what is less obvious is how best to facilitate critical thinking in an unpredictable and connected world. This became apparent with the disappointing finding that undergraduate students in higher education were not developing reflective thinking abilities (King and Kitchener 1994). The reason for this is that, invariably, undergraduate education has been characterized by passive information dissemination lectures with their inherently limited demands for academic engagement.

The reality is that there are few opportunities in undergraduate higher education for students to collaboratively explore ideas and truly test understanding through critical discourse. It has been my experience that invariably professors say their goal is to develop critical thinkers but have only a vague or idiosyncratic conception of critical thinking and certainly little appreciation of how best to instill it in their students. For many learners the emphasis appears to be on the critical at the expense of the thinking in a process of free inquiry. In the best sense of the word, to be critical is to constructively question. Another mistake is disseminating too much information without an opportunity to explore, reflect and analyze (privately and publically) what is being assimilated. There is seldom an opportunity for exploratory discourse. While we will see in subsequent chapters that this is changing, an understanding of critical thinking and how it can be developed is of central importance in higher education.

Critical thinking is seen here as rigorously analyzing, conceptualizing and assessing ideas through personal reflection and public discourse. It has been stated that critical thinking is not a separate activity from inquiry or collaborative learning (MacKnight 2000, p.38). To think is to question; to question is to inquire. Most importantly, to think is to question one's own thoughts and this requires intervention. Critical reflection is illuminated and assessed through discourse and a disciplined exchange of ideas that initiate further thought. For this reason it is important to note the integral role of critical thinking to inquiry and thinking collaboratively. Critical thinking is not a set of specific skills that can be transmitted in a classroom.

Critical thinking is a process of constructive and collaborative inquiry marked by phases of identifying the problem, exploration, integration and resolution. It is a question of being deeply immersed in resolving a dilemma or problem while collaboratively questioning conceptions and examining alternative perceptions and ideas. Moreover, collaboration without meta-cognitive awareness of the inquiry process will limit critical thinking and a deep approach to learning. We return to the concept of shared metacognition in Chapters 5 and 6.

There has been a rich history of contextual influences on thinking and learning. The earliest and perhaps the most influential from an educational perspective has been John Dewey. Dewey used the phrase "reflective thinking" in a manner consistent with critical thinking. He suggested that reflective thinking was inherently critical (Dewey 1933). Moreover, he saw it as a core educational aim and argued that it deepens the meaning of our experiences and allows for continued growth (Dewey 1933). Dewey went further in suggesting that reflective thinking is central to a democratic society (Dewey 1916). When considering reflective thinking, it is essential that we recognize that Dewey rejected any separation of the individual and society; the world of ideas (psychological) and the world of experience (sociological) are organically fused. Reflective thinking was to make connections or conceptualize the relationships between experience and ideas.

For Dewey, the best way to realize reflective thinking was through inquiry. He believed that there is no greater defect in education than the "failure to secure the active co-operation of the pupil" (Dewey 1938, p. 67). Reflective inquiry is central to construct meaning and knowledge from experience. A key principle of a worthwhile educational experience was interaction, particularly in the form of "free communication" (Dewey 1916). Reflective thinking is the method of an educational experience and this method was the generalization of the scientific method – the phases of which are suggestion, diagnosing the suggestion or problem, developing a hypothesis, exploration, and verification. Finally, Dewey suggested that it was also essential to possess the disposition to be open-minded; that is, to consider other possibilities and be prepared to be wrong. This transactional process he called practical inquiry and it is the genesis of thinking collaboratively and the cognitive presence model described in Chapter 4.

Pedagogically, the educational challenge for Dewey (1933) was: "How shall we treat subject matter that is supplied by textbook and teacher so that it shall rank as reflective inquiry, not as ready-made intellectual pablum to be accepted and swallowed just as if it were something bought at a shop" (p. 257). In essence, it is the same challenge we face today that Dewey faced a century ago. How do we engage the learner and avoid leaving the individual to his or her own devices? As individuals we are likely to be unaware of, or rationalize, contrary information to produce plausible explanations while avoiding dissonance and uncertainty. Circular arguments and discussions with one's self do not shake erroneous beliefs or offer novel insights. Most individuals stay with existing beliefs unless challenged. Therefore the essential role of discourse is to encourage the critical examination of personal meaning and the reason for thinking collaboratively. Reflective or critical thinking is dependent upon free or open communication and purposeful engagement in collaboratively testing personal meaning and building mutual understanding.

Another researcher that directed our attention to socially situated thinking and reflective inquiry was Vygotsky. Vygotsky provided an important perspective on the social origins of the thinking individual. He believed that "both individuals and society are mutually produced and reproduced" (Wells 2000, p.55). The extension of Vygotsky's view is "the notion of learning as a process of inquiry" (Lee and Smagorinsky 2000, p. 6). According to Vygotsky (1978), high level cognitive functioning is first manifested interpersonally (i.e., collaborative discourse) from which the individual creates meaning. An inherent expectation of the inquiry process is that individual meaning is open to negotiation through discourse. The Vygotskian perspective calls for "reconstituting classrooms and schools as communities of inquiry" (Wells 2000, p. 61). We explore this notion of a community of inquiry that frames our discussion of thinking and learning collaboratively in Chapter 5. However, before we can do this we need to clarify the foundational constructs of a community of inquiry.

Collaborative Constructivism

Collaboration implies a shared activity. For this to be successful, collaboration requires a sense of shared purpose and mutual interdependence in achieving intended learning outcomes. There is growing evidence as to the benefits of collaborative approaches to higher-order learning (Cecez-Kecmanovic and Webb 2000; Garrison and Archer 2000; Johnson and Johnson 2009). The conditions, however, for collaboration in a learning environment are complex. Collaboration in a learning context is predicated upon open but focused communication if personal meaning and mutual understanding are to be constructed. With regard to focused communication, it should be noted that collaboration is different from cooperation in that the latter represents individual contributions to a common task without the shared influence from members of a group.

Constructivism is a critical approach to constructing personal meaning from experience. In education, constructivism has largely replaced the simplistic and mistaken view that knowledge is transmitted from the teacher to the student. As Prawat (1992) states, "in all constructivist teaching-learning scenarios, the traditional telling-listening relationship between teacher and student is replaced by one more complex and interactive" (p. 357). The constructivist approach focuses on individuals constructing meaning and making sense of new experiences by integrating them with prior knowledge. To do this, learners must take it upon themselves to think critically and creatively. However, constructing personal meaning is not an autonomous activity. The essence of constructivism is authentic communication. As such, personal meaning is best constructed in collaborative settings where misconceptions can be detected and challenged.

As noted previously, critical thinking is conducted in the rational domain and from the perspective of individual rationality. However, reflective inquiry is more than rational and logical thinking. Socially situated and distributive cognition is one area that looks at cognitive processes beyond the mind of the individual. Brown *et al.* (1989) argued that "knowledge is situated, being in part a product of the activity, context, and culture in which it is developed and used" (p. 32). This perspective has an enormous influence on our understanding of thinking and learning collaboratively. It recognizes that internal cognition can be shared and shaped by external influence. From the perspective here, the interest is in how individual cognitive processes (constructing meaning and confirming understanding) are influenced in a collaborative learning environment; or, more specifically, how do the activities, context, and culture of a community of inquiry influence thinking and learning?

Socially situated cognition is consistent with and grounded in the work of Vygotsky's social origins of thinking. Vygotsky believed that knowledge evolves through interaction mediated by language. Subsequently this socially situated view of cognition led to the collaborative constructivist perspective that learning in an educational sense should be based in an environment of critical discourse (Garrison 2013). The particular focus here is how cognitive processes are distributed in a community of learners. Discourse in a purposeful community of inquiry can lead to understanding, not necessarily agreement or consensus. That is, learners can gain an understanding of different perspectives while arguing for a particular perspective. The point is to be aware of other perspectives and to be able to rationally defend a position. The collaborative constructivist perspective "provides an inherent opportunity to challenge and test understanding … [and] with broader agreement collective knowledge is realized" (Garrison 2013, p. 4). Meaning, understanding and knowledge construction ultimately depends on the quality and possibilities of the communication among a community of learners. The goal is to come to some form of shared understanding or at least an appreciation of the issues and ideas associated with the intellectual challenge.

Learning in an educational sense is a socially situated enterprise. The key constructivist dynamics are reflection and discourse. Critical discourse is founded on skepticism and questioning (i.e., inquiry) and is the source for the development of new ideas and knowledge. In this way uncertainty is the source of inspiration and creativity. Transmission of knowledge as rigid and fixed destroys the curiosity and questioning that are essential to collaborative constructivism. Therefore, the role and state of uncertainty associated with the complexity of collaboratively constructing meaning and understanding in a knowledge society must be recognized.

Community and Collaboration

The next question is what constitutes a collaborative constructivist community of learners. First, we begin with the reality that a "basic element of human nature is that people feel compelled to belong to groups" (Wilson 2012, p. 290). Following this, a viable group or community requires identity, cohesion, and communication to address the inevitable struggle between interests of the individual and the group. The human tendency to identify and join communities with common interests without abandoning personal interests and responsibilities is the core dynamic of thinking collaboratively.

Community is defined here by purpose, interdependence and communication. The formation and sustainability of community is dependent upon identity related to common purpose and interest. In this regard, a sense of mutual interdependence and trust must be created. Only through a sense of common purpose and belonging can an environment of open communication and critical discourse be realized. A learning community has both a social and academic focus where open communication is nurtured through both cohesive social interactions and purposeful cognitive communication. Collaboration goes to the heart of community and collaborative constructivism is the core dynamic of a learning community. A learning community sets the conditions for constructing personal meaning and achieving mutual understanding.

A community values individuals for their diversity of perspectives and experience while providing the security and means to critically examine and meaningfully reconstruct these perspectives. The group provides the means to select the best ideas and actions that serve all members. As we have learned from an evolutionary perspective, thinking collaboratively simply outperforms that of the individual. The characteristics of common purpose, communication and diversity of ideas found in a community provide the essential means and advantage to think collaboratively. These are the basic characteristics of a community of inquiry that we use as the framework to more fully explore thinking collaboratively, both theoretically and pragmatically.

A truly collaborative learning experience raises practical challenges of considerable complexity associated with the nature of the transaction between and among the participants. Interaction does not mean there is collaboration (Zhao *et al.* 2014). A transactional learning experience suggests a recursive, collaborative and mutually beneficial experience. Of particular importance for a transactional thinking and learning experience is a social presence that offers open communication to facilitate collaborative inquiry. This welcomes divergent perspectives and ideas, which lessens the risk for ideological ruts. Dewey (1916) recognized the importance of collaboration when he noted that community is based on common interest with communication being its essence. However, for purposes of educational inquiry, communication must be sustained over a period of time to develop the necessary trust for purposeful collaboration.

Thinking collaboratively recognizes the open nature of inquiry. True inquiry is unpredictable, which necessitates that discourse be allowed to explore new ideas and paths of interest. Educationally these digressions are constrained by time limitations and therefore directional decisions must be made with awareness as to the intent of the learning experience. These strategic decisions reflect the importance of leadership in a community of learners. The success of thinking and learning collaboratively is the insights associated with the goals of the group. Leadership judgments are crucial to ensure that intended goals remain in focus, while leaving open opportunities to constructively digress to explore relevant perspectives and ideas. However, this cannot be delegated to one person but must be distributed across the group if the true nature of thinking collaboratively is to be realized.

Formal education is a collaborative thinking and learning experience where the leadership, goals and timelines may be more clearly defined. However, the fundamental characteristics of an informal collaborative experience are the same. In both formal and informal learning experiences participants share a common goal, engage in open communication, and welcome insightful leadership. The primary risk in an informal learning experience is the issue of leadership and focus, while the risk in a formal learning environment is excessive deference to the designated instructional leader. The issue here is that, at some point, participants must collaboratively take responsibility for creating a sense of community, committing to its goals, and agreeing on the dynamics of the inquiry. Diversity of perspectives and ideas may be essential for productive collaboration, but leadership is essential to sustain focus and achieve the intended outcomes. Rational discourse must welcome disagreement but it must be expressed thoughtfully and with respect. Thinking collaboratively is dependent upon leadership to shape cohesion and commitment to the process of critical inquiry.

Collaboration is essential for a learning community that creates the conditions where we can share and explore ideas through discourse that may be contrary to individual perspectives and beliefs. Discourse is the key to thinking collaboratively due to a limiting cognitive state of the individual that is referred to as confirmation bias (Nickerson 1998). Confirmation bias is the propensity to unconsciously ignore contrary evidence in order to maintain a previously held belief or perspective. The fact is that most of us "generally like to avoid personally disquieting information" (Nickerson 1998, p. 176). As such, we selectively see what we are familiar with or wish to see and subconsciously reject ideas and evidence that may challenge our prior views of the world. Left to our own devices, it is virtually impossible for the individual to objectively examine the credibility of his or her beliefs. Inevitably this requires others to put a metaphorical mirror to our thinking so we can see our ideas more objectively.

The rationale for thinking collaboratively begins with the need to address confirmation bias. In the long run confirmation bias is clearly a maladaptive tendency that is best addressed through critical and collaborative approaches to thinking and learning. We must safeguard against uncritically selecting familiar ideas and/or rejecting ideas consciously or subconsciously because they do not conform to currently held beliefs. The dynamic must be a rational process where members of the group are encouraged to collaboratively and critically explore (find new relevant ideas), interpret (relate to previous ideas), challenge (question accepted truths), and integrate thoughts (create new ideas) into more satisfactory interpretations of our experiences. This is the process of thinking collaboratively and the means to avoid unwittingly selecting evidence to defend existing beliefs without examining alternative ideas or hypotheses.

Thinking collaboratively describes the fusion of the reflective world of the individual and the connected world of the group. This fusion of thinking and collaborating is the beginning of community. In a community of inquiry an environment is created for participants to better manage academic challenges and cognitive tasks through collaboration. Social presence focuses on the communication and cohesion dimensions that allow participants to engage collaboratively and constructively to address confirmation bias. Collaboration in terms of being supportive to others has been shown to positively influence one's perception of competence and achievement (Purzer 2011). Leadership, however, is the core enabling element that keeps the community focused on task and open to new ideas.

Collaboration and Competition

At this point it is worthwhile to digress somewhat to understand the corrosive nature of competition in terms of collaborative construction of knowledge. Competition can undermine group cohesion and the development of a community of learners by shutting down open communication and the sharing of ideas. Competition in a learning setting limits the possibilities of being exposed to new ideas, changing misconceptions, and developing new perspectives. Critical discourse and respectfully challenging ideas has little to do with the win-lose criterion of competition and personal ego. Communities of inquiry offer contrary views of the world that stimulate collaborative thinking and learning. Such communities provide a healthy degree of uncertainty and a means to search for resolution to personal and cognitive dissonance.

An interesting study related to critical discourse and respect looked at disagreeableness in the context of sharing ideas (Hunter and Cushenbery 2014). The authors proposed that while disagreeableness may be helpful in sharing ideas in an unsupportive environment, the opposite is likely to be true in supportive environments. At the outset, the authors identify an important phenomenon associated with our concern for confirmation bias. They state that there is "research evidence to suggest that we have an implicit preference for unoriginal ideas" (second page). One reason may be that there is an added cognitive demand to analyze innovative ideas. It also may offer personal risk in terms of being negatively judged or ridiculed. As such, it is important that individuals feel secure to disagree. In this regard, Hunter and Cushenbery (2014) found that being disagreeable did not have utility in an environment supportive of original ideas. The advantage of a community of learners is that there is social and cognitive support to critically assess and understand novel ideas. Of course, a community of inquiry is considered a supportive environment for critically and respectfully analyzing innovative or challenging ideas and, therefore, an appropriate level of agreeableness, or better, respect, is an advantage in a supportive environment.

Competition that is focused on winners and losers will create disagreeable participants and undermine seeking truth through inquiry. Winning an argument is contrary to thinking and learning collaboratively. It makes no sense to think in terms of individual winners and losers if the goal is deep and meaningful learning. However, the impact on the "losers" can be enormously destructive in terms of persistence and development of successful learning strategies. Competition in learning is an isolating experience. Why would we want to learn from others if the outcome is a winner and a loser? If we do not open up our thoughts to others, we are simply caught in a self-replicating loop of thinking with no perspective on our assumptions and thoughts. Not only is it more effective to think and learn collaboratively, it is more emotionally and motivationally uplifting to be engaged with others in a worthwhile shared experience where the outcome is likely to be better than that achieved individually. It is not wise to underestimate the influence of community on motivation through the development of relationships that offer emotional and academic support, which encourages persistence when deeply exploring complex issues. An educational experience is by definition thinking collaboratively where engaging with others benefits all participants.

Too often educational contexts introduce competition through an excessive emphasis on assigning grades – most often through objective testing that measures information recall that is easy to mark. This inevitably leads to an emphasis on surface or instrumental learning. Inappropriate assessment based on competition expressed through distributing grades on a normal curve does little to encourage a deep approach to learning. To reduce this kind of competition, feedback must be formative and challenges to ideas should not be seen as personal attacks. It is clear that a quality learning experience occurs when we can engage in discourse in a climate of trust where ideas can be explored and challenged without questioning the integrity or ability of participants. Thinking collaboratively is premised upon a commitment to purposeful, respectful and transactional inquiry. It is a matter of creating deep approaches to learning, constructing personal meaning, and achieving shared understanding (not necessarily agreement). The result is personal and shared knowledge and attitudes that can lead to further opportunities for intellectual growth and contribution to societal knowledge.

Even when the structural purpose is competition, such as a sporting event, the best results are achieved when it is not seen as a personal competition. That is, one tries to achieve a personal best and learn how to improve through the competition. While this may sound unrealistically ideal, the fact is that personalizing competition undermines performance in the long-term. Success in a sporting event, or learning, is best achieved when the focus is on one's own performance. This may have been best demonstrated by the exceptional golfer Jack Nicklaus. Most often he was only focused on his performance and played against the course. Competition was internal and he tried not to be distracted by unconstructive feedback from his opponent. He did not concern himself with what his playing partners were doing. If they played better he was the first to congratulate them. This approach certainly allowed him to stay in the moment which maximized his performance. So, even in structurally competitive situations, it is advantageous to be motivated by internal expectations and not external competition. Perhaps more to the point, when preparing for a structurally competitive situation, preparation is inevitably best done collaboratively with coaches and other players to discover ways to maximize performance. Note that we talk about players as participants and not villainous competitors. We believe that this should be the essence of sport and learning in the best sense.

Metacognition and Regulation

Thinking and learning is not just about constructing knowledge. The thinking and learning process also includes acquiring effective learning strategies and attitudes that help guide and persevere in resolving an issue or problem. Thinking collaboratively encourages individuals to think about their thinking. One cannot engage in thinking collaboratively without having our thoughts reflected back. Sharing one's thoughts and taking part in collaborative learning activities necessitates that learners take responsibility to construct meaning and confirm understanding. Acquiring these abilities is greatly assisted in a community of inquiry where the insights of others can inform productive intellectual approaches and strategies. Such collaborative inquiry leads to enhanced metacognitive awareness and an ability to learn to learn and continue to learn.

To be a reflective thinker, one must be prepared to think about the process of thinking. Although we have described the increasing awareness of socially situated and distributed cognition, metacognition has largely been a study of the awareness of the individual about his or her thinking. Surprisingly, only in recent years has metacognitive research specifically focused on thinking and learning in shared environments (Chan 2012; Cho and Kim 2013; Garrison and Akyol 2015; Iiskala *et al.* 2011).

The search for meaning in higher education requires high levels of critical thinking and inquiry. Critical thinking and inquiry is predicated upon the ability of learners to construct personal meaning and confirm shared understanding. In a collaborative constructivist approach to thinking and learning, this ability is dependent upon an appreciation of the inquiry process. Metacognition is described here as awareness of, and ability to regulate, the inquiry process. Moreover, regulation of thinking and learning is controlled through the executive processes of monitoring and managing inquiry. Such metacognitive descriptions, however, do not explicitly reflect the nature of thinking and learning in collaborative environments. Metacognition in a community of learners must include the awareness and skills to monitor and manage the inquiry process of self and others (described more fully in Chapters 5 and 6).

In a collaborative thinking and learning context, metacognition must mediate between individual cognitive functions and collaborative learning activities. While it is not often explicitly recognized in definitions of metacognition, the importance of sharing cognitive experiences has been made clear (Schraw 2001; Wade and Fauske 2004; White *et al.* 2009). Flavell (1987) states clearly that metacognition is congruent with needing "to communicate, explain, and justify … one's thinking to self and others" (p. 27). The ability to discuss an idea and engage in collaborative tasks needs to be central to a metacognition construct (Larkin 2009). That is, thinking collaboratively must incorporate a shared metacognitive process.

Metacognition integrates the functions of teacher and learner. In a learning community participants are expected to take on the role and responsibilities of both learner and teacher. Teaching responsibilities are not the exclusive function of one individual, although initially the instructor of record in a formal learning context will take the lead. As time goes on, various individuals should begin to take increasing responsibility for providing teaching presence based on their knowledge and expertise. While the teacher and instructor may well offer greater subject and pedagogic expertise, each participant must take responsibility for learning and leading which means developing metacognitive awareness and ability.

Summary

The key to prospering in a connected knowledge society is to be able to think and learn collaboratively. Creativity and innovation does not happen in a vacuum. Thinking collaboratively avoids the risk of group-think. The goal to thinking collaboratively is to develop expectations and a climate where ideas can be challenged without feeling threatened. This perspective is further developed through collaborative inquiry and the construct of thinking and learning in a community of inquiry. Collaborative inquiry is realized by social constructivist approaches to learning and developing metacognitive awareness of the process of disciplined inquiry.

From an educational perspective, collaboration is essential for the development of critical thinking and learning. The primary case for thinking and learning collaboratively is made by humans' natural tendency to hold on to previously held beliefs regardless of contrary evidence. Our tendency is to see the familiar and subconsciously reject disrupting ideas and information. As individuals it is virtually impossible to objectively examine the credibility of our beliefs. We need the feedback of the group to mirror our thoughts, expose flawed thinking and inject contrary ideas to be a catalyst for critical analysis. This is the critical and creative dynamic of thinking and learning collaboratively.

However, before we can understand the role of learning communities in greater detail, we need to explore the affordances of information and communication technologies that have greatly expanded the possibilities for thinking and learning collaboratively through ubiquitous connectivity and sustainable communities of inquiry.

3
TECHNOLOGY AND THINKING

> ... technology may enframe and colonize; but it may also liberate repressed potentialities of the lifeworld that would otherwise have remained submerged.
>
> (Feenberg 1999, p. 222.)

While we know that information and communication technologies are transforming the world of work and leisure, the challenging question is: how are they changing how we think and learn? What are the technological innovations that are impacting thinking and learning? What can communication technologies offer us that may be disruptive educationally? What thinking and learning possibilities present themselves that were not apparent or available previously?

We begin this exploration with a focus on new and emerging technologies that can engage students in reflective and collaborative approaches to thinking and learning. At the outset, we must be clear that technology can connect or distance people. The key is to understand that: "Simply capitalizing on new technology is not enough; the new models must use these tools and services to engage students on a deeper level" (*NMC Horizon Report* 2014, p. 26). The premise and argument here is that to engage thinkers on a deeper level is to engage them in collaborative, transactional approaches. In this regard, technology makes possible connected communities that can be sustained over time and space.

Technology can mediate cognition and collaboration. Technology, however, does not inherently determine the approach to thinking and learning.

While its attributes clearly influence possible applications, the real importance is the creative approaches and designs that support thinking and learning collaboratively. This focuses us on the affordances of technology with regard to its communication possibilities, which provide opportunities for communication and collaboration. That is, the ability to stimulate reflection and sustain discourse. It is the thoughtful application of technology that builds communities of learners that engage in thinking collaboratively.

Technological Innovations

Technological innovations are a powerful disruptive influence in terms of how we approach thinking and learning. But do not be misled by the seductive influence of technological gadgetry. We must be clear as to what approaches and transactions can improve (perhaps transform) the thinking and learning experience. Technology must serve worthwhile thinking and learning experiences and goals. In this regard, what can communication technologies offer approaches to thinking and learning?

Information and communication technologies (ICT) are general purpose technologies that are pervasive, improve over time, and spawn new innovations (Brynjolfsson and McAfee 2014). The insight from our perspective is that ICTs are going to increase their influence on thinking and learning positively or negatively. In the positive sense they can help create the conditions for discourse and the creative integration of ideas. However, it must be recognized that they can also create the conditions for mindless interaction. It is not just being connected to new ideas through ICTs but engaging in the collaborative exploration and the integration of these ideas that spawn new insights and innovations. This is summarized in the following way:

> The next great meta-idea … has already been found: it can be seen in the new communities of minds and machines made possible by networked digital devices … The GPT [general purpose technologies] of ICT has given birth to radically new ways to combine and recombine ideas.
>
> *(Brynjolfsson and McAfee 2014, pp. 79-80.)*

This speaks to the essence of thinking collaboratively. Being able to connect with others and share ideas is an enormous catalyst for thinking and learning critically and creatively. However, not all sharing of thoughts can be considered deep and meaningful learning. This is clearly evident with the proliferation of social media. The pervasiveness and popularity of social networking in such a relatively short period of time is astonishing and has an enormous influence in shaping communication. This stunning influence on how we communicate has caused many of us to reflect on the nature and quality of thinking and learning.

The important question is what role might social media have on thinking and learning collaboratively? Social media does a very good job of staying in touch with friends and sharing personal interests and activities. The reality is that spontaneous and superficial messages do not encourage depth of thought and sustained discourse. While they do serve a purpose, social engagement does not equate to scholarly engagement. Educational discourse is more than sharing pictures and opinions. Part of the problem is that it has been "found that university students do not really have deep knowledge of technology" (Kirschner and van Merrienboer 2013, p. 170) and, more importantly, "learners neither are skilled in information problem solving … nor have the expertise needed to determine what they do not know and what they, therefore, need to learn" (p. 177). This should be a sobering thought about our understanding of communications technology and, specifically, about how we are using technology for thinking and learning.

The danger is that the Internet and social media are encouraging ideological cocooning. It allows one to live within a set of assumptions and beliefs without challenge. It has been shown that those who use social media are more reluctant to express dissenting views to friends and colleagues. In a recent study, Hampton *et al.* (2014) found a reluctance to speak out on social media if others did not share their views. The reality is that we are most willing to express our thoughts and read messages from those to whom we agree. At the basis of this is that most of us seek the approval of others, especially if they are acquaintances. As a result, on social media, one is likely to be exposed to like-minded people and the perverse reinforcement of one's biases. This creates the great danger of unwarranted certainty while reducing the incentive and influence to think critically and collaboratively.

The age of social media therefore increases the risk of confirmation bias; that is, an avoidance of contrary perspectives and facts. Social media and networking play into confirmation bias where assumptions and facts are not open to challenge. This point was made by Malcolm Gladwell (2010) when he discussed weak and strong-tie interpersonal connections. Social media are built around weak-tie connections that are essentially a "leaderless organizational system" not particularly good at directing and focusing discussion and challenging assumptions. He speaks of weak-tie systems or networks as having the characteristic of interactivity but an "inability to arbitrate." This reflects a lack of critical focus and leadership. The main reason for this is that there are no real inter-personal connections and common goals. There is a lack of purposeful engagement where assumptions and ideas are challenged. In essence this represents a form of group-think.

Dron and Anderson (2014) make this same point when they argue that large-scale social media "are not designed with learning in mind and tend to use and magnify implicit or explicit preferences/actions rather than target learning needs" (The Stupidity of Mobs, 5th paragraph). The point is that participants in these "crowds" are driven by their own narrow interests and limit participants to what they already know. They are not challenged or introduced to new perspectives and associated ideas. While there may be interaction at a superficial level, there is no real thinking. That is, thinking that takes us out of our comfort zone and encourages us to make sense of the glut of information that bombards us.

On the other hand, strong-tie connections typical of small groups are characterized by trust, coherence and commitment. A purposeful learning community is an example of a strong-tie connection where participants have common interests and goals as well as personal connections. With social media there are no deep connections, purposeful focus, or group cohesion. Therefore, there are serious limitations in using social media as a forum for deep and meaningful discourse. Social media do not have the commitment or leadership necessary to facilitate and direct critical reflection and discourse. Sustained discourse and commitment to thinking collaboratively is very difficult in an environment of 140 characters. It has inherent structural constraints and is the antithesis of a purposeful community of inquiry. There are, however, technologies that can be used to create and sustain powerful learning communities where membership requires commitment, focus and purposeful engagement; a community where access to information (breadth) is fused with critical thinking (depth) for the purposes of deep and meaningful inquiry.

Educators should rightly be skeptical of the value of the technologies that are shaping our society. A recent study found that educators believed that learning networks were the most important technological application, while stating that social networking was the least important (Prichett *et al.* 2013). This suggests that educators are correct in questioning the type of interaction that can add educational value. Few educators have made use of social media such as Twitter and perhaps for good reason. Being connected does not guarantee or even encourage constructive interaction. Its goal is to capture attention and entertain, not engage participants in thinking deeply through reflection and discourse. Social media is what it says – social. It is not called "thoughtful media" for good reason. Its purpose is social amusement and it is therefore limited in terms of purposeful thinking and learning. On the other hand, some social media such as blogs and wikis have been used to engage students in meaningful discussions and to conduct worthwhile group projects. Social media have clearly changed the way people interact and share experiences (*NMC Horizon Report* 2014), but we must be critical as to its contribution to engage learners in meaningful discourse and thinking collaboratively.

The skepticism of incorporating social media into the classroom can be balanced with technologies that are intriguing from a learning perspective. Learning analytics has been identified as a technology that will have an important impact in higher education (*NMC Horizon Report* 2014, p. 26). Learning analytics look at learner data (data mining) for the purpose of informing learning strategies. The challenge is to measure things that are valued and important to the educational experience. From our perspective this means assessing discourse and advanced thinking. Learning analytics become a real possibility and advancement in guiding communities of learners where the goal is purposeful and meaningful thinking and learning. The reason is that analytics can be used to understand if students are engaged in thinking and learning collaboratively; or if one individual is dominating the discussion and limiting thoughtful participation. This will allow educators to become more innovative in terms of how we design learning experiences that address thinking collaboratively in complex technological learning environments.

When exploring the role of technology, it is also of interest to explore the possibilities of artificial intelligence (AI), especially when combined with the benefits and possibilities of data mining (big data). To be clear, intelligent machines will not be taking over the creative construction of knowledge. Yes, AI will be able to help us analyze complex situations and sort through massive amounts of information, but the novel integration of ideas remains a uniquely human experience that is best complemented by collaboration with other insightful human beings. Thinking collaboratively can make use of AI but this must include the unique abilities and perspectives of other purposeful thinkers and learners. The risk is that we unthinkingly experience life through the latest technological development. The algorithms of AI can be powerful tools but relying on them to make sense of our world is to risk a determinist existence. The bottom line is that we must understand what we gain (and lose) educationally with AI and similar cutting-edge technological tools.

As Dyens (2014) states, "Education in the 21st century must be built upon the premise of the human–machine entanglement" (2nd last paragraph). But this is premised on an understanding of what is unique to human thinking; and what is unique is the social nature of living and learning. At the core of social learning environments is open communication and collaboration that encourages critical and creative thinking. We must be able to create an environment of thoughtful and engaged learners; but ones that understand and can capitalize on the particular advantages of communication technologies while maintaining that which is uniquely human. In essence, technology is a mediator between teaching and cognitive presence (not unlike social presence). Thinking can be mediated and may even be necessitated by technology, but we must not lose sight of the importance of deep connections with human beings. It is through such connections that we fully expand the unique capabilities of human intelligence.

That said, digital technologies and intelligent programs are changing how we approach learning. The intelligence of tutoring systems and, to a lesser extent, gaming, provides a valuable form of interaction and feedback. However, it is important to appreciate that these applications are more a form of engagement with pre-defined content than they are critically exploring new ideas and lines of reasoning. The goal should be integrating these individually focused applications with discourse and collaborative activities. Intelligent tutoring systems are evolving and will be able to simulate high level interaction; however, identifying misconceptions and offering explanations in complex areas of study represent a serious limitation. Perhaps, then, the replacement of intelligent, creative and motivational human beings may not be an ideal we should be striving to achieve.

Networks allow us to connect people through technology that can control various devices remotely but also sustain person-to-person communication. Connecting people is only the beginning. The real challenge is shaping the nature of the interaction made possible by the technology. Computers may provide access to information but they do not construct new ideas or ways of doing things – people do. Routine tasks can be left to computers but innovative thinking is still the domain of individuals engaged in stimulating environments; environments where individuals think critically and creatively in collaboration with others. Access to information may allow individuals to construct personal meaning but critical discourse provide the means to construct new ideas. While there are many advantages to face-to-face interactions, ubiquitous and sustained mediated communication offers possibilities that we are only beginning to understand. The challenge is to distinguish between frivolous and thoughtful communication.

While technology is a disruptive influence, it will not be educationally transformative unless we address the assumptions of a worthwhile thinking and learning experience and define more precisely what the nature of that experience should be. It is argued here that if the nature of thinking and learning is to be deep and meaningful, then it must be collaborative and constructive. While it is clear that communication technologies have the potential to engage learners through stimulating reflection and discourse, we need a more precise understanding of thinking and learning enhanced or made possible through the adoption of communication technologies.

Technology-Enhanced Approaches

To be sure, information and communication technologies are increasingly important elements in the educational environment. Technology is disrupting and shaping how we approach and design educational experiences – mostly for the better. One of the most positive disruptions is the displacement of the information dissemination model represented by the ubiquitous lecture. Access to information is no longer the primary challenge for educators. The educational challenge and goal is information literacy and learning to critically make sense of an avalanche of information we are exposed to in a connected world. So the important question now is: how are communication technologies changing the thinking and learning experience? How do educators perceive technology with regard to the place of face-to-face learning experiences in a pervasive virtual world?

Communication technologies are bringing people together in new and enhanced ways, not all educationally worthwhile. From an educational perspective we need to understand how these technologies add value beyond entertainment and amusement. This necessitates an understanding of the communication characteristics embodied in the technology that enhance thinking and learning collaboratively. We begin by exploring the differences in oral and written communication. This is addressed by Feenberg (1999) who states that writing is not a poor substitute for speech, "but another fundamental medium of expression with its own properties and powers" (p. 345). For example, verbal discourse may be appropriate to begin exploring a subject but writing can allow us to rigorously review and refine ideas through objective reflections that are not time dependent. These same ideas can then be revised based upon feedback. Verbal discourse does not provide equal opportunities for participation or have the same clarity of expression and opportunity for revision. The obvious point is that there is a place for both oral and written communication when used for appropriate purposes.

Written or text-based communication is inherently asynchronous. That is, there is some period of time to think about what one is going to write before creating a permanent record for others to read, reflect on and respond. Writing slows down the production of the message for the benefit of more insightful, researched and crafted communiques. It also reduces cognitive load and memory demands with the immutability of content and access to additional online information. The significant shift pragmatically is the integration of focused online discussion boards where learners are able to continue discourse through text messages after class or work collaboratively on group activities regardless of time and location. More importantly, I would argue that written discourse may well be suited to the development of deep and meaningful approaches to learning through deductive and focused tasks. The challenge is to understand the properties and powers of both oral and written communication and how they can best be integrated if we are to design optimal thinking and learning experiences. Regardless, the point is that we provide diversity in how we share our thinking. Both oral and written communication can externalize our thinking but in different ways that meet different needs.

Before the digital age, the educational transaction was largely conducted orally, most often in the form of a lecture. The problem is that synchronous oral communication is fast-paced, spontaneous but also ephemeral. Oral communication has advantages in setting a climate for collaboration but it is not conducive to reviewing and reflecting on what was said. Students are left to the distracting and imperfect task of taking accurate notes with little opportunity to think about what is being said. More often than not, the oral communication is one-way; that is, the instructor simply conveys information to the students. Oral communication by way of a lecture is great for inductively exploring ideas and generating commitment to an intended task. However, although oral communication may engender greater commitment and engagement, it is less reflective and precise when compared with written communication. It also limits opportunities to question and share new ideas. To be clear, while we must remain skeptical of technological innovations, they do expand opportunities to engage in reflective discourse.

New forms of purposeful and engaged inquiry are being made possible by emerging communication technologies. To address the limitations of a particular means of communication, an approach that has attracted considerable interest is blended learning. Blended approaches to learning integrate face-to-face and online learning experiences. This is an approach to designing thinking and learning experiences that optimally integrates the strengths of fast-paced verbal communication with reflective written communication (the proportion of each depending on disciplinary and educational needs). As a result, there is enormous potential for the thoughtful fusion of synchronous and asynchronous forms of communication that is multiplicative, not additive in its benefits for thinking and learning collaboratively.

The concept of blended learning may seem intuitively apparent but there is no one template for its design. The reality is that blended learning represents a fundamental redesign (i.e. it goes beyond enhancing lectures with optional online discussions) that transforms traditional information-focused education. Inherent to a blended learning design is enhancing the interaction and engagement of the participants for knowledge construction by using innovative learning technologies. This means creatively designing reflective and collaborative learning experiences that utilize communication technologies for particular thinking and learning purposes. The possibilities include flipping the traditional approach by introducing students to the content of the lesson online (through a recorded lecture, reading assignment or online tutorial) before class. Then students come to the class having read the material or listened to a presentation and are prepared to engage in a meaningful discussion. This opens the possibility to use the class time to engage the learners in discourse and to challenge and refine their understanding of the subject matter. Sustained discourse and designing group activities beyond the classroom become possibilities. In many situations this can have the added administrative benefit of reducing the number of scheduled classes while academically increasing the opportunity for thinking and learning collaboratively. Blended learning is discussed more fully in the next chapter.

Another approach reliant on technology that has gained surprisingly widespread attention is Massive Online Open Courses (MOOCs). Why so much attention has been directed to MOOCs is not entirely clear. The primary reason would appear to be access at reduced cost. It surely cannot be qualitative improvements. Qualitative deficiencies evidenced by the enormously high dropout rates of MOOCs are not surprising when we consider its lack of purposeful engagement. To be clear, the learning approach advocated here is not compatible with massive online courses. It should also be noted that MOOCs are not new. They are essentially independent study approaches that provide efficient access to content and have been with us since the early days of distance education. The unremarkable feature of MOOCs is access to content but with limited opportunities for interaction and collaboration. In this way they are distance education courses updated by replacing the mail system with course content downloaded from the Internet (see the next chapter for further analysis).

Summary

Approaches to thinking and learning are being transformed as ubiquitous communication technologies emerge in all aspects of society. Technology allows us to move from accessing information to engaging in higher order learning activities. That is, to have opportunities to collaboratively construct and confirm meaning of complex phenomena through the possibilities of sustained virtual learning communities. Technology can support new approaches to teaching and learning where students acquire the skills and abilities that will be needed in a connected knowledge society. Those skills will most certainly be associated with the ability to think and engage with others. To accomplish this goal would be to concentrate "… on the relationships that surround the enactment of the design … along with a basic understanding of the role that the technology or infrastructure play in the teaching and learning process" (Jones *et al.* 2006, p. 52). That is, it is the nature of the relationships among the participants and the communication possibilities reflected by the technological affordances that will shape the thinking and learning experience.

The issue is not that we can connect people, but how we connect people. The challenge for educators is to understand technology to the degree that it can "liberate repressed potentialities" (Feenberg 1999, p. 222). The true potential of information and communications technology is creating learning communities where thinking and learning collaboratively can be sustained. In other words, the creation of a collaborative learning environment that extends thinking possibilities through connections made possible by technology. Innovation in thinking and learning has often had technology as its catalyst. Engagement can be greatly enhanced and is sometimes entirely dependent upon technology. Technology can be a transformational force in causing us to critically examine how we think and organize learning experiences.

Let me end with sage advice from a colleague of mine, Phil Ice, about predicting future technological innovation in education. He notes that the accuracy of prediction is about 10 percent after five years. The important insight that he offers, however, is that while predictions of specific technological applications are not realized, conceptual frameworks often are realized, albeit often in a manner not envisioned (Ice 2010). The point is that we need to focus on educational purposes, arguments and frameworks with regard to seeing the technological future with regard to thinking and learning. The future of technologies in education will inevitably reveal themselves through the lens of approaches to thinking and learning. To this point, we must keep in mind our educational ideals, while recognizing the opportunities and limitations offered by existing and emerging information and communication technologies.

4

A NEW ERA

The new digital technologies have altered meaningfully the operation of campus-based and distance teaching universities worldwide and have offered exciting opportunities to enrich learning environments.

(Guri-Rosenblit 2014, p. 113.)

Information and communication technologies are significantly reshaping both distance and campus-based educational organizations. In the first decade of this century the Internet and the World Wide Web have moved from interaction with content to interaction with people. This has focused our attention on the possibilities for thinking and learning collaboratively. The ability to support sustained discourse beyond the classroom is transforming the educational experience. It is now possible to create cohesive learning communities where open, sustained discourse takes precedence over information transmission and self-directed approaches to learning.

The distinct advantage of digital technologies is the capability to connect teachers with students and students with students without the restrictions of time and space. Time and space has become unbundled and discourse can be sustained over time regardless of distance. Moreover, with asynchronous communication, time slows with distance (educational relativity of time) and participants have time to reflect before responding. Written asynchronous discussion and the relativity of time become a significant asset. The permanence of text offers a distinct form of educational discourse that encourages thoughtful exchanges. Exchanges can be read, re-read and revised based on evidence and feedback. Verbal discussions are ephemeral and linear while online text-based discussions are concrete and are able to simultaneously accommodate multiple voices.

Distance Education

Historically, distance education was encoded in print-based learning packages provided to students through the mail system. The problem, however, was that the message never changed, regardless of the student's interests or questions. In other words, there was little opportunity for diagnosing misconceptions and providing corrective feedback. The primary feedback was a grade on an exam if students did not drop out before getting to that stage. For these reasons, traditional distance education was described in terms of an industrial production model. Otto Peters (1994a) in the mid-1960s analyzed the operational characteristics of distance education and noted the organizational structure was designed to achieve economies of scale through self-instructional print packages.

Distance education at the time was necessarily predicated upon an autonomous approach to learning. Teaching and learning issues were dictated by the technologies available at the time. The result was an approach that "reduces the forms of shared learning, and keeps learners away from personal interactions and critical discourse" (Peters 1994b, p. 16). However, the limitations of this approach from a teaching and learning perspective were noted by some researchers at the time (Garrison 1989). Notwithstanding the dominance of the industrial paradigm and the espoused ideal of the autonomous learner, the limitations with regard to interaction and feedback were a critical deficiency. Some tried to finesse this limitation with the concept of "guided didactic conversation" that relied on simulated conversation in the pre-produced course package (Holmberg 1989, p. 43). However, this proved to be largely a rationalization for the lack of real two-way communication (written or verbal).

Making the learner as autonomous as possible resulted in an extremely high dropout rate. The United Kingdom Open University (UKOU) reported that "only one in five of its new students ever end up with a degree" (Woodley and Simpson 2014, p. 460). It should be noted that the UKOU rate was one of the higher completion rates for the mega distance education institutions (i.e., large scale industrialized operations). Considering these results it was difficult to rationalize, let alone idealize, the autonomous and self-directed learner in an open distance system. Moreover, an *open* distance education institution accepts students without prior qualifications.

For this reason student preparation is very likely to be inadequate and high dropout rates should not be surprising.

While students attend a distance education institution for a variety of reasons, it has been argued that high dropout is associated with the nature of the connection and the lack of teaching presence that students have with the institution (Garrison 1987; Garrison 2000). It was argued that the key variable in understanding dropout was limited communication and ease of connection. The evidence at the time and certainly more recently was that completion rates are correlated with the quality of the communication largely in terms of opportunities for interaction and feedback. To argue, as traditional distance educators did, that interaction with an institution through the course materials can replace a teacher is not supported by the evidence. While there has been no comprehensive explanatory theory of dropout in distance education to date, it is suggested here that it is very much associated with teaching presence and particularly with a collaborative thinking and learning experience that academically engages students.

In attempting to understand and address the implications of limited interaction and support, some began to take a more critical view and noted two-way communication as an unavoidable defining feature in any educational transaction (Garrison 1989). This began a shift in thinking from immutable structural issues to transactional or process issues (Garrison 2000). Garrison and Shale (1990) made this point in the title of their book *Education at a Distance*. This was an attempt to "avoid the restrictive trap of describing distance education based upon its existing forms and structures" (p. 25) and break loose from the organizational assumptions and constraints of the industrial model. This shift in point of view also opens the door to understanding new communication technologies from the perspective of how they could support two-way communication. This was not widely accepted at the time but proved to be prescient in terms of recent developments and the emergence of collaborative approaches to education generally.

Campus-Based Education

With the growth of higher education and accompanying class sizes in the last half century, we saw an increasing reliance on the lecture. More students had to be accommodated and the default became "teaching" (really talking to) literally hundreds of students in a lecture hall. This was a means to transmit information verbally in the form of a lecture. It was the students' responsibility to absorb as much as they could through note taking and making sense of the information largely on their own. One might ask how verbally transmitting information to passive listeners in a lecture hall is different from or more advantageous than transmitting information via print in traditional distance education. In neither situation are students provided with an opportunity to cognitively engage with others and diagnose or clarify a misconception – except in the exam when it is too late for any meaningful constructive or formative feedback.

No feedback

From a research perspective, the reality of this situation was confirmed repeatedly when the results of no significant difference were found each time distance education outcomes were compared with those of campus-based education. That is, learning outcomes showed no difference regardless of whether the experience was virtual or face-to-face. Unfortunately, what was not recognized was that these were comparisons of information recall. For information recall why would one expect that one method would necessarily be superior to the other? Both were deficient in that they only emphasized memorization and recall. Similar passive information distribution approaches based on the individual trying to assimilate a massive amount of content largely on their own is not going to be advantaged by any particular method of disseminating that information. In both distance and campus-based situations students had to individually rely on reading the information and absorbing it as best they could. Asking questions was difficult in either context and neither had the opportunity for meaningful discourse.

The recognition of a need for change crystalized at the turn of the twenty-first century. Increasingly it was realized that there was a disconnect between current educational needs and past practices that persisted despite advances in communication technologies and an increasingly connected society. The relevance of higher education has been challenged by the communication revolution and the need for critical and creative approaches to thinking and learning. The reach of technology is changing higher education in "the way we organize ourselves, our policies, our culture, what faculty do, the way we work, and those we serve" (Ikenberry 2001, Foreword). Faculty are also increasingly expected to use technology to engage their students. Engagement is seen as embracing the full cycle of practical inquiry that goes beyond exploration and includes resolution of real problems and testing through practical application. In response to the demands of a knowledge society there is a focus on thinking collaboratively through sustained discourse whether that be synchronous verbal or asynchronous written communication.

The classical theory of paradigm shifts (Kuhn 1962) points out that there are periods when new paradigms emerge that challenge traditional assumptions and ideas. The idea that challenged the passive information assimilation approach to learning was the idea of learning communities that could actively engage learners in collaborative inquiry. The new communication technologies made possible collaborative thinking and learning approaches not imagined in the old paradigm. One of the first significant challenges to the old paradigm in higher education was provided by Boyer (1990) who advocated the "scholarship of discovery" as a form of disciplined inquiry. The important point is that learning in higher education should be active investigative activities, not passive information assimilation. Learning should be reframed as consisting of discovery, integration, application, and teaching – a classic form of inquiry. Information was to be interpreted and integrated into existing knowledge and, through application, new ideas could be tested as to their validity and usefulness. Finally, the scholarship of teaching and learning was about intellectual engagement with others and developing mutual understanding. Learning was considered a collaborative dynamic to actively stimulate critical and creative thinkers. Of course, for those who were familiar with Dewey's work, these were familiar ideas.

With the influence of Boyer, the idea of actively engaging students in their learning emerged strongly in the first decade of this century. Engagement was intended to improve approaches to teaching and learning through more active and deeper approaches to learning, through increased effort, and collaborative problem solving and feedback (Kuh 2009). The goal was to develop the predisposition and ability to continue learning. As is often the case, the commitment to engagement emerged in a significant manner when an instrument, the *National Survey of Student Engagement*, was developed that could provide an objective measure of engagement and student success (Kuh 2000). Two of the key measures were active and collaborative learning and student-faculty interaction. This survey made possible a means to measure the extent of interaction across an institution and it created much discussion about how best to promote engagement.

Many institutions began to think about collaborative approaches and developing learning communities. Of interest here is a recent study of the relationship between engagement and learning communities that was based on the recognition that learning communities are related to student success at college (Pike *et al.* 2011). They concluded "that learning community participation was positively and significantly related to student engagement" (p. 300). However, the benefits appear to depend on the nature of the learning community and the type of engagement. This is not surprising and what makes a learning community work in terms of the type of engagement and intended learning outcomes is explored more thoroughly in the next chapters.

While the shift from passive to engaged approaches for thinking and learning have been more transformational than revolutionary, significant changes in this regard are on an exponential curve. Technology has certainly precipitated change but the driving force is what learners do, more so than what teachers do in front of the classroom. Instructor performance is taking on a very different meaning as it shifts from a presentation to a facilitation focus. Students of today and tomorrow must and will learn to think and solve problems through collaborative inquiry. Technology allows greater numbers of students to benefit from thinking and learning collaboratively. For this to happen, however, we must continue to focus on creating environments for thinking and learning collaboratively, while not becoming seduced by the latest technology. Educational technologies must always be judged by the quality of the learning experience.

Considering the ubiquity of technology in all aspects of our lives, we must be careful about perceptions of technology. From the learners' perspective, younger people may well appear to be addicted to social media; however, it is a myth that they are proficient with learning technologies and have a preference to learn through technology. Notwithstanding the fact that young people are immersed with technology, a recent study did not find overwhelming evidence that undergraduate "students are more prepared to use technology or that they have higher expectations of technology to enhance the learning environment than they did a few years ago" (Dahlstrom and Bichsel 2014, p. 9). Students in higher education are critically discerning about technology and when it makes sense to use it. While students may well see technology as useful in their social lives, they do not necessarily see it as a useful tool in their educational lives – nor should they.

Educators are not making full use of the technology for learning purposes even though students say that technology does engage them more in their courses. A good example is that undergraduate students reported that course management systems were the most used learning technology but only "56% have used it in most or all of their courses" (Dahlstrom and Bichsel 2014, p. 10). The message is that undergraduate students are open to using technology in meaningful ways but a significant number of faculty do not seem to be onboard. It would appear there is still considerable technological reluctance to use technology and we have some way to go in terms of the effective use of technology. Moreover, it is argued here that the use of technology has more to do with academic leadership and understanding the importance of engaging learners than student resistance. In this regard there is a crucial role for faculty development.

More research is needed to determine the specific circumstances under which students would like their "living technologies" to be adapted as "learning technologies". With regard to living technologies, it would appear that the social preference of millennials (the digital generation) "… is to be able to connect their virtual lives with their physical lives" (Gutfreund 2014). That is, social media is enhancing and not replacing the social experience of the digital generation. There is still an inherent desire for face-to-face human interaction. The same is true for their preferences with regard to an educational experience. The entrepreneurial world has accepted the need to engage their consumer (White 2014), and it is clear that educators must learn the same lesson to fully engage the millennial student. For sound educational and social reasons, the passive and autonomous learner in higher and distance education is facing a limited life. The way forward educationally with regard to integrating our real and virtual worlds is online and blended approaches to learning.

Online Learning

Technically speaking, online learning is communicating for the purposes of learning through networked computers. For educational purposes this form of computer-mediated communication is largely focused on asynchronous written communication, although it can support both asynchronous and synchronous text, verbal and graphic communication. Online learning offers the possibility to collaboratively engage learners independent of time and distance. However, distance education is not the genesis of online learning, nor is online learning simply a more expedient form of distance education. Online learning evolved out of the field of computer-assisted instruction and specifically computer conferencing. With the maturation of the Internet, the focus of computer conferencing was on two-way communication and, with that, offered new possibilities for engaged learning.

The collaborative features of online learning created a collision of worldviews regarding the industrial model of distance education (Garrison 1997b). Online learning represented an accessible opportunity to think and learn collaboratively at a distance. As a result, distance education institutions are confronted with an existential challenge. As Evans and Pauling (2010) argue, the future of distance education will depend on how it adapts to the new technology or "it will be off to the scrap yard" (p. 216). At the same time it should be noted that the large open distance education institutions do serve many adult learners who for socio-economic reasons do not have the qualifications or the time to study full-time or in a campus-based context. In such situations, distance educators must make compromises to meet these socio-economic constraints. For example, practical realities in the developing world are likely to preclude wide-scale adoption of online learning. However, in the developed world, the adoption of more interactive and engaged approaches is the challenge for most distance education institutions.

Peters' industrial description of distance education was a post-facto description of its organizational delivery, not a defense of this learning paradigm. This is a major reason why online learning researchers have largely ignored the distance education literature (Evans and Haughey 2014). Consistent with Kuhn's description of paradigm shifts, it has become very uncomfortable for distance education researchers to confront the reality of a significant shift in thinking about the theory and practice of distance education. Distance learning today is capable of providing interaction with independence in a way that was unthinkable just a few decades previously. The adoption of the interactive possibilities of online learning represents a new category of learning at a distance and has created the need for "a total overhaul of the very basic characteristics of the industrial mode of distance education" (Guri-Rosenblit 2014, p. 116).

Online learning is having a similar disruptive effect in higher education. It has reinforced the attention to be directed to more collaborative approaches to learning and is transforming campus-based higher education institutions. Interestingly, this transformation is a form of restoration of higher education typified by small classes and discourse. Online learning makes possible a return of the historical values placed on meaningful discourse in small groups of learners. This is reinforced with the somewhat surprising finding that "students in online learning conditions performed modestly better than those receiving face-to-face instruction" (Means *et al.* 2009, p. ix). Notwithstanding this finding, one of the strongest arguments for online learning in higher education is its integration with the strengths and preferences for face-to-face learning experiences.

Blended Learning

Blended learning has been described as "the organic integration of thoughtfully selected and complementary face-to-face and online approaches and technologies" (Garrison and Vaughan 2008, p. 148). Beyond the obvious integration of real and virtual worlds, the term "organic" reflects being grounded in the specifics of practice. Each situation is unique and so should be the specifics of the blended design. Therefore, considerable thought must be given to the disciplinary demands, participant abilities, and contextual constraints. For this reason, there is no standard template for designing a blended learning experience. Each situation must be carefully considered as to how to blend classroom and online learning experiences based on any number of contextual factors.

The most common adoption of online learning in campus-based institutions is blending online and face-to-face experiences that increase student engagement. The vast majority of higher education institutions offer blended learning courses. A recent survey has shown that: "More than four in five students (85%) took at least a few courses that were blended (contained at least some online components and some face-to-face components) in the past year, up from 79% in 2013" (Dahlstrom and Bichsel 2014, p. 22). Considering this, it seems clear that blended approaches will be the norm in higher education as "students say that these environments best support how they learn" (Dahlstrom 2012, p. 5). It will become increasingly difficult to find a course that does not have some significant component of online learning and the term blended learning may well become redundant.

Considering the need to uniquely adapt to the contextual demands, blended learning invariably represents a fundamental rethinking of traditional approaches. It is a shift in focus to what the learner does to construct meaning while concurrently having faculty move from presenters and performers to leaders of the inquiry process. However, simply adding optional and often trivial online discussions does not meet the threshold for worthwhile blended learning. This only adds extra work without addressing deficiencies in how we approach learning – be they a lecture or reliance on autonomous study materials. Students are beginning to demand greater access to the professor and blended learning is a practical way to provide this. Blended learning provides a means to rethink the educational experience from the perspective of building learning communities that will support collaborative thinking and learning effectively, efficiently and conveniently.

Blended learning designs cut across disciplines and apply to large and small classes as well as undergraduate and graduate courses and programs. In smaller classes we can reduce lectures and replace them with structured online discourse and collaborative assignments. Large introductory courses can be enhanced with increased online discussion, computer-based assignments and timely support from both fellow students and instructors. In each of these scenarios typically half the classes are replaced with more engaged learning experiences be they small group seminars or online discussion forums. Another common blended learning example applies to graduate courses and programs that offer effectiveness with convenient access for working professionals. In this context, the course may begin with a face-to-face experience and perhaps have another face-to-face class midway; however, most of the collaborative work will be done online in variously sized groups.

New technology and approaches associated with blended learning can be challenging for most faculty. For this reason a collaborative approach to redesigning a course can be more creative, effective and motivational. Collaborative approaches to designing a blended learning course will become commonplace in higher education. Such an approach will not only offer the advantage of a variety of perspectives but provide an impetus for continued improvement. Faculty support and collaboration at the design and delivery level will provide a catalyst and support to rethink their courses from a student engagement perspective. This is dependent upon institutions offering faculty development communities where they can learn about blended designs in face-to-face and online learning environments (Garrison and Vaughan 2008). In this way, faculty directly experience blended learning while designing such experiences for their students.

Blended learning represents a win/win for the faculty, institution and students if we are careful to recognize the collaborative thinking and learning possibilities it offers. Blended learning has blossomed because it addresses important issues of effectiveness, efficiency and convenience. The typical skepticism of faculty is being overcome with examples of how it can benefit faculty and students. These advantages, however, can be eroded when institutional leadership is not apparent and effectiveness is sacrificed for efficiency and convenience. Enthusiasm for online learning must be carefully managed based upon improved learning experiences with its foundation in collaborative thinking and learning experiences. Increasing access is laudable but we must be cautious as to what we are providing access.

MOOCs

The first massive open online courses (MOOCs) attempted to form learning communities for independent learners to access information and connect to others through the Internet. They comprised reasonably sophisticated learners who could construct knowledge through the connections and collaborations they could generate through communication technologies. As a result, this type of informal MOOC proved to be limited. A more recent adaptation of the MOOC saw traditional campus-based institutions begin to explore these designs for purposes of access. These courses were open to very large enrolments without qualification and typically free of charge. Essentially MOOCs offer educational resources and learning experiences to the self-directed, largely autonomous learner. This second type of MOOC, and the one that has received the most attention, is a slightly more structured form of distance education usually "facilitated" by a renowned expert. However, it is important to examine the nature of the "instruction". Participants are able to engage online with fellow participants but, due to large enrolments, individual instructor feedback is not a realistic possibility. As a result, the quantity and quality of participation in discourse is usually very low. Optional participation in discussion forums without the expertise of a facilitator does little to ensure sustained engagement or quality discourse. In this regard, serious questions have been raised about the quality of the learning experience (Toven-Lindsey *et al.* 2015).

With MOOCs the question is what purpose they serve and what is the value added. The primary added value is access to the presentation abilities of an expert but this comes at the cost of support and formative assessment. MOOCs are not designed specifically around the strength of cohesive learning communities. Network connections do not encourage the collaborative thinking and learning made possible in structured learning communities. As a result, the question is how realistic is the expectation to have meaningful discourse with massive numbers of participants and varying interests? Feedback is largely dependent upon unfacilitated online discussion groups and automated quizzes. The lack of individual academic support with accreditation challenges can be considered to be primarily responsible for low completion rates that are estimated to be around ten percent (Featherman 2014; Liyanagunawardena *et al.* 2013). While there are more structured MOOC designs, completion rates remain low (Rodriguez 2012). MOOCs' shift to disseminating content online and away from formal teaching very much reminds one of traditional distance education approaches but with the added option of interaction, which few take advantage of in terms of meaningful engagement. In fact, most never even start an assignment (Lewin 2013). The question for an institution of higher education might be, why offer such courses?

Beyond the basic question of what purpose do MOOCs serve, the important educational question is related to the nature and quality of the learning experience it offers. In particular, what effect does the size of a MOOC have on thinking and learning collaboratively? Little research has been directed to assessing MOOCs and virtually none has been done with regard to quality of the learning experience. One study, however, did attempt to get at the quality of the MOOC learning experience through the reflections of two students enrolled in two types of MOOCs (Raffaghelli *et al.* 2014). Using the CoI framework to analyze the students' reflections, the study found that their perspectives seemed to "converge in the idea of the participants' 'isolation' … [and] the effort required to make sense of their learning experience" (p. 133). It was concluded that the students "found a massive structure where only self-directed learning could lead to genuine learning outcomes" (p. 133). These learning experiences are expected considering the size of MOOCs and go to the heart of their inherent limitations from the perspective of thinking and learning collaboratively.

From this account it can be concluded that MOOCs reflect a stark contrast to learning in communities of inquiry. Communities of inquiry are characterized by purposeful and transactional learning experiences with an invaluable teaching presence that is shared by all participants. This inherently collaborative learning experience is contrasted with the large scale informal learning network of a MOOC. While participants in a MOOC are expected to assume the responsibilities of teaching presence, the non-completion rate of MOOCs reminds one more of the mega open distance education institutions. In either situation students are largely self-directed and there is no meaningful coherent learning community. Coming back to the theme of this book, it could be argued that the risk for confirmation bias increases as the size of the group grows and feedback in the form of teaching presence is reduced. Therefore, the larger the network, the less chance there will be a focus on thinking and learning collaboratively that has the potential to challenge confirmation bias. Dron and Anderson (2014) have noted the challenge in mitigating confirmation bias in large scale networks. They note the difficulty "to provide structured courses beyond the institution such as large-scale MOOCs … where it is all too easy to become lost in social space" (Dron and Anderson 2014, p. 12). Participants in MOOCs have trouble identifying sufficiently with large groups such that they will take the opportunity to engage in critical discourse and contribute to thinking and learning collaboratively. In short, participants in MOOCs do not feel a strong connection, loyalty or responsibility to other members of the network. As the dropout data suggests, this lack of connection severely risks group cohesion and persistence. In turn, the lack of group cohesion can only reduce the quality of the discourse (i.e., thinking collaboratively) and the learning experience.

While campus-based educational institutions are beginning to address access and affordability issues (traditionally the domain of distance education), distance education institutions are exploring more interactive online learning designs. Interestingly, both campus-based and distance education institutions are beginning to recognize and explore how to have both access and engagement. While there is an apparent convergence of these two historical approaches, neither appears to fully appreciate the implications in adopting large scale online learning. Access cannot trump meaningful engagement if effectiveness is the goal. MOOCs essentially are not new nor will they prove to be disruptive in higher education. This is evidenced by distance education moving away from the questionable idea of learner independence by integrating collaborative approaches to thinking and learning. The move toward thinking and learning collaboratively has just begun to play out.

MOOCs have been described as revolutionary and the future of higher education. The reality, however, is that MOOCs are an example of reinventing traditional distance education with new technologies. They are trying to replicate the efficiencies of traditional distance education with the unrealistic and unfulfilled promise of interaction among the participants. In massive open learning contexts, teaching presence is diffused to the point that it barely functions. Students enrolled in a MOOC are as isolated as were traditional distance education students who relied on a prescribed self-directed learning package, and with no better chance of getting credit for their efforts. It makes one wonder if those promoting the adoption of MOOCs would be as enthusiastic if they had a better understanding of the history of distance education and its limitations. While MOOCs have brought welcome attention to online learning, the reality is that "MOOCs will be seen as a limited-purpose tool that conveys limited benefits in a limited set of contexts" (Wasson 2013, p. 194). In summary, it has to be concluded "that many MOOCs are poorly designed, have insufficient quality control and are not well managed at the point of delivery" (Online Learning News 2015).

Integration of online learning in face-to-face and distance education represent different challenges. Campus-based institutions can actually gain both effectiveness and efficiency by adopting online learning (e.g., blended approaches), while distance education institutions will exchange cost-efficiencies for enhanced effectiveness through increased student engagement. The legacy of MOOCs will be the attention they brought to online learning and the move to blended learning. The ongoing challenge is to focus on the quality of the educational transaction and how online learning can support communities of inquiry and thinking collaboratively.

Summary

Distance education institutions were very much shaped by approaches that attempted to maximize the independence of learners through the assimilation of information organized and packaged industrially by large institutions. It was often repeated that institutions were doing the teaching. Distance education emerged to meet larger socio-economic constraints that restricted individuals from attending a campus-based institution. Unfortunately, distance education practices based on print and mail delivery made it impossible for students to engage in meaningful discourse or be exposed to unexpected information and experiences. Students were simply exposed to content that responded to questions by repeating the prepared answer that was designed into the learning package.

The shifting focus of higher education on to inquiry and engagement is attempting to address passive approaches such as large lectures. The development of ubiquitous communication technologies and the Internet proved to be the catalyst for rethinking campus-based approaches largely represented by the lecture. This opened the era of online and blended learning where distance was not a barrier but an unprecedented asset and complement to face-to-face learning experiences. Communication technologies represent the opening of enormous possibilities to engage learners synchronously and asynchronously at a distance. The risk, however, was to focus too much on the latest technology and not ensure that the nature of the learning experience was driving innovation.

A new era of education is being shaped by a rethinking of the traditional passive and independent approaches to learning. The need for more engaged approaches is being recognized and addressed as we continue to evolve as a connected, knowledge society. It is no longer acceptable to rely on information dissemination techniques for education when access to information is ubiquitous and immediate. On the other hand, online and blended learning possibilities are making engagement in collaborative thinking and learning practicable and desirable. Online and blended learning designs provide more engaged inquiry strategies reflected by a fusion of reflection and discourse.

The inherent bias for most individuals to reinforce existing ideological positions brings us back to the central theme of facilitating critical thinking and learning that will result in critical discourse and meaningful learning outcomes. It is argued here that the creation of learning communities that provide sustained possibilities for collaborative thinking and learning experiences will transform teaching and learning. The guiding framework in exploring and providing direction in this regard is explored in the next chapter.

5

THE COMMUNITY OF INQUIRY

... education by inquiry demands collaborative effort; traditional lecturing should not be the dominant mode of instruction ....

(Kenny 1998.)

Thinking collaboratively is best understood and practiced in a community of inquiry. More specifically, the Community of Inquiry (CoI) framework provides a context to fully explore and understand the construct of thinking collaboratively and its practical implications (Garrison 2011). The CoI framework consists of three interdependent core elements – social, cognitive and teaching presence. This framework represents a collaborative approach to inquiry that fuses personal reflection and shared discourse for a deep and meaningful learning experience.

Communities of Inquiry

Matthew Lipman (2003) popularized the term "community of inquiry" in the 1980s when he and his colleagues began to rethink educational practice from the perspective of a reflective paradigm. Lipman believed that while critical reflection is the objective, it is socially situated. Lipman's reflective paradigm is grounded in the work of John Dewey and his concept of inquiry. Dewey (1938) believed that inquiry is central to reflective thinking and indispensable to the educational transaction. For Dewey, inquiry is the process of creating knowledge. Communities of inquiry *today* ✱

provide intellectual challenges and the environment for individuals to stretch their depth and breadth of thinking and learning through collaboration. In today's context, we argue that communities of inquiry are critically important to learning to adapt and succeed in a connected, knowledge-driven society.

In our connected world there are a myriad of ways to create and sustain learning communities. Communities of inquiry make use of the technological affordances of a rapidly evolving digital society to create the conditions for sustained discourse where the breadth of access to information can be fused with the depth of collaborative inquiry. Educators have the potential to take advantage of the connectivity of the digital world and actively engage learners in collaborative thinking and learning experiences. A functioning community of inquiry enhanced by communication technologies is central to sustained inquiry expressed by reflection and discourse (thinking collaboratively).

The concept of community draws our attention to the social nature of

Similar interests ✱

inquiry. In a technologically connected society, the community dimension is defined by the identity of the participants in the group, not the physical location. That is, participants identify with why they are members of the group – the purpose for the group's existence. It is a place to connect with others who possess similar interests and goals. In short, community displays the characteristics of common purpose, interdependence, collaboration, communication, and trust. A connected community is essential to sustained inquiry and the potential to realize the benefits of thinking and learning collaboratively. It provides the conditions for participants to exchange ideas, sustain discourse, collaboratively construct meaning, and validate knowledge. A welcoming climate provides the environment for the concomitance of reflection and critical discourse that is the core dynamic of a community of inquiry. A community of inquiry provides the security and guidance for thinking collaboratively – a place where personal meaning is put into the public arena for critical consideration.

Dewey recognized the inseparability of the public and private worlds and explored this unity through the concepts of community and inquiry. He believed that for an educational experience to be both socially worthwhile and personally meaningful, it needed to be manifested through the fusion of reflection and discourse. Constructing personal meaning and developing shared understanding evolves in an environment of discourse. Thinking collaboratively has its genesis in this perspective that unites the individual (reflective) and shared (collaborative) worlds. This is consistent with Vygotsky's social constructivist approach to education and his "notion of learning as a process of inquiry" (Lee and Smagorinsky 2000, p. 6). This reinforces the central role of inquiry and thinking collaboratively in the CoI framework.

Vygotsky, like Dewey, believed it was a great mistake to focus on outcomes at the expense of process. The CoI framework is a process model that focuses on free inquiry where participants are not constrained by confirmation bias and where they learn as much about the inquiry process as they do about the content being studied. Inquiry cannot be fully predictable and the exclusive focus on predetermined outcomes will inevitably restrict open communication, critical discourse, and the development of metacognitive awareness (learning how to learn). In short, the focus on outcomes reinforces the impression that knowledge can be transmitted from the teacher to the student in whole, which Dewey categorically rejected. The risk of an outcome focus is that outcomes will take precedence over the means, at the cost of meaningful discourse and deep understanding. Finally, it is the proper responsibility of the educator to establish the conditions for the learning transaction. While educators do establish and attempt to measure intended outcomes to a degree, deep and meaningful outcomes are often unpredictable and difficult to assess. The greatest assurance of quality learning outcomes is to ensure a deep and meaningful learning experience through collaborative inquiry.

The philosophical foundation for thinking collaboratively has been described as collaborative constructivism. The reason for this is that we believe this terminology properly places the dynamic of thinking collaboratively between the more extreme "radical" and "social" constructivist philosophical positions. That is, it suggests a better balance between the cognitive and social demands of an educational experience. As such, collaborative constructivism more accurately describes the cognitively focused but socially shared activity of a purposeful thinking and learning experience. Collaborative constructivism reflects the fusion of the external and internal dynamics of a shared learning experience. The term "collaboration" addresses the transactional dynamic of a community of inquiry and the twin demands of an educational learning experience to be personally meaningful and socially worthwhile. Collaboration necessitates open communication that values respectful discourse, rational argument, and mutual understanding. Constructivism, on the other hand, embraces the individual's responsibility to create personal meaning. Thinking collaboratively from a collaborative constructivist perspective is, therefore, facilitated through integrated and balanced cohesive social transactions and purposeful cognitive discourse.

Inquiry = reflection and discourse

Inquiry is a collaborative approach to problem resolution that transpires in the context of reflective discourse and interactive questioning. Consistent with Dewey, inquiry is a process of critical reflection and discourse based on the generalized scientific method for resolving problems. It is a flexible transaction where existing knowledge and experience is subject to questioning, interpretation and transformation. It is a nonlinear process where individuals iteratively and imperceptibly move between the personal world of constructing meaning and the shared world of confirming understanding. While inquiry may be a pathway to understanding and knowledge, there is no certainty or permanence in resolving questions through inquiry. The ends become useful inputs to be tested and transformed in a continuous process of inquiry. Inquiry transforms previous knowledge and experience and this becomes material for future inquiries. That is, resolutions are immediately exposed to further questioning as the inquiry cycle begins anew. In this sense ends and means are indistinguishable.

Inquiry is socially situated and dependent upon a community of inquiry. Inquiry embedded in a learning community is focused on collaboratively exploring problems, constructing meaning, and validating understanding. The alternative of an individual thinking in isolation would sentence the individual to live within a set of assumptions and beliefs without challenge. Unchallenged thinking makes possible the avoidance of contrary perspectives and ideas and is antithetical to the transactional notion of inquiry. Inquiry is a collaborative constructive process that avoids ideological cocooning and is the model for thinking and learning collaboratively.

Inquiry can be greatly enhanced through the technological affordances of the digital world, which can help avoid ideological bias. Manifested in an environment of open communication, inquiry does not reinforce one's biases by conveniently avoiding contrary perspectives and ideas. Inquiry embedded in a purposeful learning community provides the conditions for individual ideas to be evaluated objectively through sustained critical discourse, where breadth of access to information made possible by the Internet is fused with the depth of critical reflection and discourse. This is the essence of thinking collaboratively operationalized through practical inquiry in a community of learners. In short, inquiry is the means of thinking collaboratively with the goal of a deep and meaningful learning experience where understanding is made more credible through critical thinking and discourse.

Before leaving the topic of inquiry, it may be of interest to focus on reflection as this is most often associated with learning. Recently, much has been made of the importance of collaboration and engagement. Dewey believed that thinking and acting are inseparable. He states that the nature of an educational experience "can be understood only by noting that it includes an active and passive element peculiarly combined" (Dewey 1916, p. 139). Neither thinking nor discourse "can be subordinated to the other or neglected ..." (Dewey 1959, p. 20). In fact, they are inseparable in a personally meaningful and educationally worthwhile learning experience. Although thinking in an educational context is preceded and followed by some form of discourse, thinking inevitably involves creating and capitalizing on periods of silence. *need silence.*

Deep Approaches to Learning

One of the great insights into learning in higher education is the research done on deep and surface approaches to learning. This research was pioneered by Marton and Saljo (1976) and further developed by Entwistle (Entwistle and Ramsden 1983). Marton and Saljo described surface and deep approaches as two distinct levels of information processing. Surface learning is where the student takes a reproductive or rote memorization approach to learning; while deep learning is where the intended approach is to comprehend the information and integrate it with existing knowledge structures. The construct of a deep approach to learning is the essential thinking and learning experience of the CoI framework.

While deep learning would seem to be an obvious goal of an educational experience, many educators are not fully appreciative of its practical implications. A deep and meaningful approach to learning necessitates a learning environment highly associated with two important principles. First, that the curriculum content and workload be reasonable such that it will allow students the time to process information at a deep and meaningful level. Simply put, demanding that students cover an excessive amount of information or course content ensures that students will take a surface approach. This inherently lessens opportunities for critical reflective and communicative engagement. The reality is that we cannot cover all the content in any domain of knowledge in any case. Therefore, it is essential that educational leaders focus on the structure of knowledge and the big ideas of the discipline.

The second principle relates to assessment. That is, if we wish students to approach learning at a deep level, we must assess at that level. If the rewards are to simply assimilate and recall information, students will approach learning at that level. Understanding will not be the primary goal. For most students this is the most critical issue to encourage a deep approach to learning. Rowntree (1977) reflects this when he states, "If we wish to discover the truth about an educational system, we must look into its assessment procedures" (p. 1). In short, assessment must be congruent with the level you wish students to approach their learning. Students are generally not motivated to spend their time on something that is not recognized and rewarded.

One other practical issue in supporting a deep approach to learning is diagnosing misconceptions. In this regard, the collaborative nature of a community of inquiry provides the opportunity for reflection and discourse to expose misdirected thinking. A community of inquiry creates the conditions where learners are encouraged to take deep approaches to learning through thinking and learning collaboratively. The conditions of a community of inquiry provide an opportunity for learners to make sense of new information but to also share this meaning with others such that assumptions and beliefs can be challenged and validated. As we shall see, academic leadership is crucial in thinking collaboratively and achieving deep and meaningful learning outcomes. The inquiry process is essential to thinking collaboratively and supporting deep approaches to learning. This requires further explanation and is explored more fully in the next section.

The Community of Inquiry Framework

The Community of Inquiry (CoI) is a coherent and descriptive framework that describes a collaborative and constructive approach to thinking and learning (Garrison 2011). The CoI provides a theoretical framework in which to study and understand the influence of a purposeful learning environment on the cognitive processes of the individual. This is accomplished through the concurrent consideration of three interdependent elements – cognitive, social, and teaching presence – operating in the broader context of a number of exogenous variables such as the technological means of communication. While the CoI framework was initially developed to provide an ordered understanding and a methodology to studying and practicing online learning, it is not limited to online learning. It is a generic framework derived from and having particular application to higher education, although there is no reason it could not be easily adapted to any form of thinking and learning collaboratively. The following diagram (Figure 5.1) is a map for thinking and learning collaboratively. It reflects the operational elements and their intersections that result in a deep and meaningful collaborative learning experience.

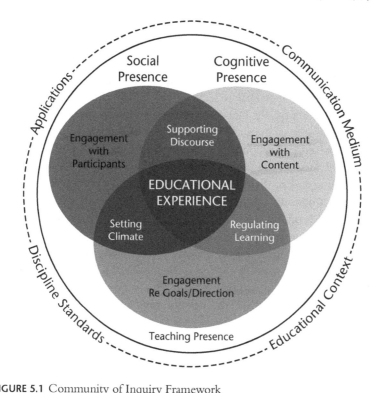

FIGURE 5.1 Community of Inquiry Framework

The benefit of the CoI framework is to help us understand thinking and learning collaboratively. When the CoI framework was first developed, we focused on inquiry as the process to achieve deep and meaningful learning (Garrison *et al.* 2001). Consistent with Dewey, we assumed that thinking during the inquiry process is mediated by both psychological and sociological influences. While both cognitive and social presence influence the quality of the learning experience, it was also clear that in an educational context leadership (teaching presence) is also an essential condition for transactional inquiry to be conducted effectively and efficiently. The tripartite CoI framework has been consistently validated in a range of studies since its inception and is widely used to understand and study collaborative and technologically mediated learning environments (Garrison 2011).

The core thinking and learning element, cognitive presence, is operationalized through the Practical Inquiry (PI) model. Practical inquiry is a multi-phased process initiated by a triggering event and subsequently moving through a recursive process including phases of exploration, integration and resolution. The PI model is two dimensional (see Figure 5.2). One dimension, deliberation-action, reflects the psychological (private) and sociological (shared) components of inquiry. The first dimension reflects the opportunity for personal reflection which is then shared and further reflected upon recursively. The second dimension, perception-conception, reflects that aspect of inquiry that occurs at the cusp of the reflective and shared worlds. This contrasts the divergent process of perception and analysis of ideas with the convergent process of conception and synthesis in constructing and confirming meaning. The boundary of the perception-conception dimension is where thoughts are shared and molded collaboratively. The PI model represents a picture of the complex process of constructing meaning reflectively and negotiating understanding collaboratively. The PI model has been cited as suitable for assessing critical thinking (Buraphadeja and Dawson 2008) and is the model of thinking and learning collaboratively. It should also be noted that metacognitive awareness of the inquiry process is crucial for the development of thinking and learning collaboratively.

To reiterate, inquiry is a collaborative dynamic. For this reason it must be supported in an environment of open communication that reflects the contextual conditions for thinking and learning collaboratively. Social presence is the second core element of the CoI framework and is defined as "the ability of participants to identify with the group or course of study,

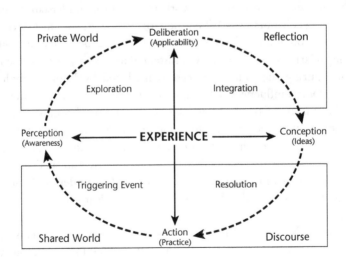

FIGURE 5.2 Practical Inquiry Model

communicate purposefully in a trusting environment, and develop personal and affective relationships progressively by way of projecting their individual personalities" (Garrison 2011, p. 34). This definition conveys the dynamic nature of social presence in progressively developing a community of inquiry. Social presence is first focused on the purpose of the inquiry (identity to the group) and then on ensuring the conditions for free and open communication within the group. Only then is the foundation for group cohesion established. The third developmental aspect of social presence, personal relationships, should be allowed to grow naturally over time to further enhance open communication and cohesion. However, it must also be recognized that interpersonal relationships have the potential to limit open communication if personal relationships inhibit open communication. For this reason the focus must first be on group identity and cohesion established in an environment of open and free communication.

The CoI framework inherently recognizes the social nature of humans and the motivation to connect socially with others. It is clear that a sense of belonging contributes significantly to motivation. What is often lost in the exploration of a cognitive process such as thinking collaboratively is the motivational and emotional dimension. Motivation is an emotional response that has an enormous mediating influence on thinking in a community of inquiry. Motivation is essential in precipitating interest and directing and sustaining effort (volition). As such, motivation can have considerable influence on initiating and sustaining cognitive activities. There is an emotional reward and cognitive advantage for thinking collaboratively in a community of inquiry. This is the intrinsic satisfaction of constructing meaning and being recognized as a contributing member of the learning community. It has been shown that learning in a community of inquiry is inherently satisfying and leads to perceived learning (Garrison 2011). The key for sustained motivation and emotional satisfaction is for participants to identify with the purpose of the learning community and experience a climate where they feel they are valued participants.

Teaching presence is the third element and the key to a successful and sustained community of inquiry. A purposeful learning transaction requires leadership. Teaching presence provides the essential leadership dimension that keeps a learning community functioning effectively and efficiently. It consists of three progressive responsibilities – the design, facilitation, and direction of cognitive and social presences. Facilitation and direction are essential to ensure that discourse does not prematurely converge or inappropriately diverge. The concept of teaching (not teacher) presence is intended to suggest that all participants of a community of inquiry must assume the appropriate level of responsibility, based on their knowledge and ability, for constructing personal meaning but also for shaping the discourse of the group. In a collaborative thinking and learning environment this is not the sole responsibility of the formally designated instructor, although the disciplinary and pedagogical expertise of instructor will justify direct intervention in a timely manner. The active engagement and proportional contribution of all participants is required. It should also be noted there is growing evidence of the importance of teaching presence in terms of perceived learning and satisfaction (Garrison 2011). The distributed responsibility for teaching presence has enormous implications for thinking and learning collaboratively, including the development of metacognitive awareness essential to monitor and manage thinking individually and collaboratively.

Before we leave this overview it is important to emphasize the progressive and developmental nature of the CoI framework, both within and among the presences. Figure 5.3 provides a breakdown of the categories that constitute each of the presences. But this is only the categorical description of their constitution. What is equally important is that the emphasis on these categories evolves over time. While each category is present and they impact the learning experience in a concerted manner, the focus will shift over time. For example, the first priority in a community of inquiry is to establish the conditions for open communication (e.g., trust). In turn, open communication then can create group cohesion. While interpersonal relationships need to be addressed early through introductions and collaborative activities, it must be recognized that these relationships take time to develop and are not the prime focus of the participants in a formal learning environment. The dynamic and progressive nature of cognitive presence, however, is inherently easier to recognize in terms of its developmental phases. Upon reflection it will also become apparent that the focus of teaching presence categories or responsibilities also shifts as students get deeper into a course of studies. The first task of teaching presence is designing and organizing a deep and meaningful learning experience. During implementation, the focus on design gives way to facilitating exploration and discussion, which then shifts to more direct instruction as the resolution of specific tasks is addressed. None of these, however, are linear. They are all recursive and loop back on themselves depending on the particular challenges the group face. For example, design issues will continually arise as needs and interests evolve.

The previous paragraph is a description of the fluid nature within each of the presences. However, as we shall see in the next chapter, the focus on the presences as a whole will shift as the learning experience evolves.

ELEMENTS	CATEGORIES	INDICATORS (Examples only)
Social Presence	Open communication Group cohesion Personal/affective	Risk-free expression Group identity/collaboration Socio-emotional expression
Cognitive Presence	Triggering event Exploration Integration Resolution	Sense of puzzlement Information exchange Connecting ideas Applying new ideas
Teaching Presence	Design & organization Facilitating discourse Direct instruction	Setting curriculum, methods Shaping exchange Resolving issues

FIGURE 5.3 Community of Inquiry Categories

For example, at the beginning of a course greater attention has to be directed to social presence; but as learners become more comfortable and deeply engaged in the content the focus will shift to cognitive presence. Then, as the challenges grow, there is likely to be an increased emphasis on teaching presence to ensure that intended goals are achieved. Finally, navigating through the inquiry dynamic brings our attention to metacognition and its function in higher order learning.

Metacognition

Historically, metacognition has been largely studied from the perspective of the individual. However, with the growing interest in learning communities and shared cognitive experiences, there is an increasing focus on recognizing both individual and collaborative regulatory processes. This growing interest in thinking and learning collaboratively has been a catalyst to investigate shared metacognition.

It has been stated that the overarching goal of a community of inquiry "may be described as constructing another level of awareness—the metacognitive" (Kennedy and Kennedy 2013, p. 18). This represents identifying with the purpose and participants of the community. Others have also conceptualized metacognition on personal and shared levels when problem solving in a collaborative environment (Kim *et al.* 2013). Accordingly, when individuals are interacting with others in a collaborative learning environment, metacognition cannot be solely explained by individual conceptions. This is supported by Iiskala *et al.* (2011) who have considered metacognition in terms of a product of interaction between an individual or individuals and a surrounding context. Furthermore, it has been argued that the ability to understand and respond to others' mental states is as important as understanding one's own mental states – and they have a direct impact on each other (Son *et al.* 2012).

A community of inquiry invites a consideration of the awareness of how we think and learn collaboratively. To engage in inquiry necessitates being able to regulate learning in terms of monitoring and managing thinking and employing corrective strategies. This challenge is greatly enhanced when thinking and learning collaboratively. The practical inquiry process describes the iterative and interdependent transactional dynamic between the individual and learning community. Discourse plays an essential role in metacognitive awareness and regulatory strategies. Thinking collaboratively in a community of inquiry requires shared metacognitive awareness. Shared metacognition has been operationalized through the constructs of self and co-regulation of cognition (Garrison and Akyol 2015).

In the context of a community of inquiry, teaching presence necessitates that individuals assume appropriate degrees of responsibility to regulate learning while receiving the support and direction of the community. The goal is to distribute authority in terms of both content and procedure; that is, the instructor of record "is working toward the eventual distribution of her own role among the participants, such that each member of the group as-a-whole is capable of maintaining the double vision [i.e., epistemological and procedural]" (Kennedy and Kennedy 2010, p. 3). That is, participants in a community of inquiry are tasked with the responsibility of being a teacher and learner, and therefore they must have the metacognitive awareness of intended content goals (epistemological) and the inquiry process (metacognitive). The complexity of this challenge should not be underestimated. In this context, metacognitive awareness is the regulation of cognition that is collaboratively distributed within a community of inquiry. The construct of thinking collaboratively includes the inseparability of personal and shared regulation of learning. Thinking collaboratively extends metacognition to consider both self and co-regulatory activities. Participants in a community of inquiry are engaged with other participants' cognitive and metacognitive thoughts and activities.

Summary

We have seen that the Community of Inquiry framework has its genesis in a rich philosophical and theoretical history where inquiry is based on the generalized scientific method and a process of critical reflection and discourse. This transaction is socially situated and dependent upon a purposeful community of learners committed to collaboratively exploring problems, constructing meaning, and validating understanding. The CoI framework provides an ordered and methodological approach to thinking and learning collaboratively through the concurrent consideration of three overlapping elements – cognitive, social, and teaching presence. Understanding the dynamic nature of the three interdependent elements along with the evolving relationships among the elements goes to the core of thinking and learning collaboratively.

Just as the goal in particle physics is to unify the standard forces in nature into a grand unified theory, the goal of the CoI is to unify the elements of an educational experience (social, cognitive and teaching presences) in a theoretical framework in order to achieve symmetry among the dynamics of thinking and learning, reflection and discourse, and self and co-regulation associated with collaborative inquiry (recursively moving between the private and shared worlds). The symmetry of the inquiry process is also reflected in the reality that resolution invariably raises other questions that precipitate another cycle of inquiry. There is an elegance and authenticity in the unity of an educational experience that does not artificially separate the individual from the influences of their environment. They are inseparable and this must be recognized for a quality learning experience. In short, the CoI framework recognizes the inherent unity and symmetry of the personal and shared worlds of thinking and learning (i.e., thinking collaboratively). Anything else is to create an artificial and limited description of a deep and meaningful learning experience.

From a more immediate concern, a community of inquiry is a framework and approach that is highly relevant to a connected knowledge society. Thinking collaboratively in a community of inquiry changes how we think and learn for the better. It ensures that we consider that we may be mistaken and that we may need to examine our thoughts and beliefs through personal reflection and shared discourse. Thinking and learning collaboratively in an educational context is disruptive and transformative but it is self-correcting and the means for critical and creative thinking and preparing students for an unpredictable knowledge society. A decade and a half of research has shown the CoI framework to be a powerful tool to explore and understand thinking in collaborative learning environments. Research in this area is growing and provides new insights into and refinements of the CoI framework. It is these developments that we turn to next.

6

COMMUNITY OF INQUIRY RESEARCH

Research and theory are at the foundation of credibility and quality.

(Simonson *et al.* 2011.)

The Community of Inquiry (CoI) framework stands out as a credible and well-used educational theory that has shaped research in the exploration of teaching and learning associated with online and blended approaches to learning. A recent thematic analysis of articles and book chapters between 2000 and 2012 found the CoI framework was the most frequently cited blended learning theoretical framework (Halverson *et al.* 2013). This framework puts the focus on the educational experience and not the mediating technology. As with any theoretical framework there remains a need for continued refinement to clarify and expand our conceptual understanding of approaches to educational experiences and to help answer emerging theoretical and practical questions. Through continued refinement of the CoI framework we can better appreciate thinking and learning collaboratively in the context of recent technological disruption. The purpose of this chapter is to review the recent CoI research and emerging insights into collaborative educational experiences.

Theoretical and practical inquiry is crucial to developing the foundations that inform educational practice and guide future developments. Theory has been described as "a coherent and systematic ordering of ideas, concepts, and models with the purpose of constructing meaning to explain, interpret and shape practice" (Garrison 2000, p. 3). Theory not only reduces

What is theory?

Active

complexity and describes what is, it can also help predict emerging trends, determine what could be, and how to take effective action. As we have seen in Chapter 4, theory is invaluable in clarifying the use of terms such as online learning and distance education, as well as coping with the complexity of learning communities. Understanding the importance and practice of thinking and learning collaboratively raises the need for theoretical frameworks. Thinking and learning collaboratively can only be understood and sustained through coherent theory that is open to the very qualities it espouses – critique, discussion and confirmation. Theory is in a constant state of development; especially the indeterminate social science theories.

Information and communication technologies have raised important issues about the design and delivery of education as we enter the twenty-first century. Many of the issues associated with online learning and the adoption of technology can be attributed to the lack of research grounded in theory (Zawacki-Richter and Anderson 2014). As a result, what has become apparent is the need for a coherent understanding of educational innovations that involve technologies such that the learning experience is not defined by the technology. The challenge for educational researchers is to construct and validate a theoretical framework that will explain and anticipate educational practices across a variety of contexts and for a broad range of emerging purposes and experiences. We must move beyond hypotheticals and validate theory and practice that will capture the full potential of new and emerging communication technologies. That is, theory as an essential tool to rethink how to design relevant and meaningful learning experiences and, by providing a synthesis of concepts, capable of explaining and predicting educational developments and possibilities.

Since the 1990s research into learning has seen a resurgence led by researchers in the field of the learning sciences. The emerging field of the learning sciences is a multidisciplinary approach that begins with the premise that memorizing facts is no longer an effective educational strategy. This reflects a shift from preparing students for the industrial age to being successful in a knowledge society. The learning sciences strive for deep conceptual understanding by focusing on the active participation of learners in creative and engaged environments where they can reflectively express their state of knowledge (Sawyer 2006). Learning science research points to the importance of higher order thinking and problem solving through active inquiry. This socially situated view of learning, described as reflective discourse supported by a community of inquiry, moves education from passive "instructionism" to thinking and learning in connected and collaborative environments.

The CoI framework is strongly embedded in the learning sciences and is a direct contribution to understanding thinking and learning in a connected knowledge society. In more specific terms, the intent in this chapter is to provide an updated review of CoI research and its theoretical contributions to the field of education. This chapter will further extend the review of CoI research provided in *E-Learning in the 21st Century* that previously documented developments in the first decade since its first publication (Garrison 2011). The current review here will offer confirmatory findings and new insights into thinking and learning collaboratively. With this perspective, we turn our attention to examining evidence in support of the CoI framework and insights into thinking and learning collaboratively.

A Coherent Framework

The Community of Inquiry framework has gained considerable popularity as a comprehensive and explanatory educational theory associated with online and blended approaches to learning. It is the most widely referenced framework associated with the study of online and blended learning. More substantively, the CoI framework meets the formal requirements of a theory *theory* in that it represents a coherent set of articulated elements with defined relationships and indicators (Garrison 2011). The explanatory potential of these dynamic relationships make possible the derivation of hypotheses that can be tested and then used in the interpretation of the findings. The theoretical boundary of this framework is not limited to online educational experiences and thus represents a rich area for further research and broader application in a range of educational contexts.

To be clear, the CoI framework is not a learning theory but has adopted learning theories that provide a foundation and are consistent with collaborative educational approaches (see introductory chapters as well as Garrison and Archer 2000). The CoI framework, however, does address the why and how of a collaborative educational experience; of thinking and learning in a purposeful community of inquiry. While it is a framework that provides a conceptual structure for a collaborative educational experience, the developing understanding of the dynamic relationships among its core elements has it approaching that of a theory (set of concepts and principles intended to explain an event). We see the CoI framework as a developing educational theory that considers and explains the implications of integrating teaching and learning in a collaborative environment (see principles in next chapter). In this regard, we explore the developments of the CoI framework that serve as a valuable theoretical guide for both the study and practice of collaborative approaches to learning in an educational context.

Although research questions may be grounded in practice, they are inevitably shaped by some form of theoretical perspective. For this reason, the more coherent and comprehensive the theoretical structure, the more impactful it will be. That is, the more parsimoniously a theory can order and explain the complexities of thinking and learning in an educational environment, the more useful it will be theoretically and practically. To set the stage to consider recent validation and refinements of the CoI framework, we begin by reiterating that the framework represents a transactional deep and meaningful learning experience. As described in the previous chapter, this experience can be understood through the dynamic fusion of three presences – social, cognitive and teaching. Presence is defined as a sense of identity created through purposeful and open communication.

Presence

Significant advances in validating the CoI framework has been made possible using the CoI survey instrument (Arbaugh *et al.* 2008). This quantitative instrument has been invaluable in conducting large scale studies and factor analytic evidence has strongly confirmed the tripartite structure of the CoI framework (see Appendix A). To understand the relationships among the presences, two seminal studies have used the CoI survey to explore the causal relationships among the social, cognitive and teaching presences (Garrison, Cleveland-Innes and Fung 2010; Shea and Bidjerano 2009). In addition to validating the framework, both studies confirmed the important mediating role of social presence between teaching and cognitive presence. Moreover, it revealed the key role of teaching presence to establish both social and cognitive presence. Other studies have also found support for these relationships among the three presences (Daspit and D'Souza 2012; Jo *et al.* 2011).

The premise of the CoI framework is that an effective community of inquiry is dependent upon a holistic view of the educational experience and where its presences are in dynamic balance. This is a promising area of research. For example, Kozan and Richardson (2014) explored the interrelationships between and among the presences by controlling for the effect of the third presence. One of the important findings was; "efforts to increase social presence should not only focus on social interaction but also on encouraging cognitive presence through social interaction" (p. 72). This supports the position that participants in a community of inquiry identify first with the academic purpose of the group. As such, social presence must be developed in an environment that goes beyond social interactions and personal relationships. Social presence is created and sustained through purposeful and meaningful discourse (i.e., cognitive presence and the inquiry process) and not by focusing on interpersonal communication in isolation of the academic purpose of the community. This is explored further in the next section.

Another related area of research is how the presences in a CoI evolve in concert with each other. In this regard, it is important to understand the progressive and developmental nature of each of the constituting presences as well as the relationships among the three presences. Akyol and Garrison (2008) were the first to explore this area of interest. They found that the categories of each of the presences were clearly distinguishable and evolved essentially as theoretically hypothesized. For example, in terms of social presence, open communication indicators were high at the outset and cohesion increased over time. This is what would be expected as purposeful communication established greater cohesion and collaboration. In terms of cognitive presence, the emphasis on each of the first three phases of inquiry shifted over time as would be expected (moving from exploration to integration); however, frequency of resolution messages dropped in the final trimester. While this may appear to be anomalous, it made sense considering the final assignment was an individual project and students would not be motivated to share their thoughts of resolution. With regard to teaching presence, the categories were clearly distinguishable and theoretically understandable. Facilitation was of greater concern in the beginning but dropped as students grew in confidence and assumed greater control of the learning process. On the other hand, direct instruction increased as students moved from exploration to integration and resolution. Simply put, moving to resolution required more specific knowledge and clarity (direct instruction) with regard to the assignment. Looking at the presences in concert, each of the presences was distinguishable and performed as would be expected; that is, evidence of social presence in messages decline over time, while teaching and cognitive presence increased.

The results of the research to date have confirmed the stability of the CoI framework, although there have been attempts to add new constructs. For example, one study suggested adding an individual learner presence construct to account for self-regulation (Shea et al. 2014). However, evidence for the re-conceptualization of the CoI framework must be consistent with the premise of the framework while not creating unnecessary complexity. The foundational premise of a community of inquiry is that all participants are expected to assume the responsibilities of both teacher and student when learning in an educational community of inquiry. In addition, such fundamental changes must be based on more than the perceptions of one cohort of students. More significantly, regulation issues can be coherently and parsimoniously incorporated into the CoI framework through the shared metacognition construct (Garrison and Akyol 2015). This is a much more consistent and elegant means to deal with the issue of self-regulation. As a result, there is little rationale to fundamentally re-conceptualize the basic structure and dynamics of the CoI framework.

Social Presence

The importance of social presence is rooted in the premise that a community of inquiry reflects a collaborative, cohort-based approach to thinking and learning (a social constructivist paradigm). The term "social presence" was originally introduced by Short et al. (1976) who focused on telecommunications and a sense of intimacy resulting from a loss of physical cues such as eye contact and smiling. Their focus was largely on the quality of the medium that would allow individuals to projects themselves socially and emotionally. In the 1990s other researchers began to shift the focus from the property of the medium or technology to that of the people and their communications (largely socio-emotional) (Cui et al. 2013). Social presence continued to evolve with a shift from a focus on the affective to include interactive and cohesive responses in a community of inquiry (Rourke et al. 2001). This definition extended social presence to include communication that contributed to a sense of community and to identification with the academic purpose. The assumption was that mediated communication could develop a functional learning community through social presence.

The original CoI definition of social presence did not explicitly reflect the priority of identifying with and establishing a purposeful community of inquiry. The initial emphasis was on the socio-emotional and interpersonal relationships. While consideration of open communication and group cohesion were essential components of social presence, the overriding influence of the academic purpose of the group was not adequately addressed. Nearly a decade after the original definition of social presence was published this oversight was addressed with a shift in focus from the person to the purpose of the communication (Garrison 2009). The social presence construct was refined through a closer look at identity issues within an academic environment and the progressive dynamics of its sub-elements shifted in chronological emphasis (open communication, cohesion and interpersonal relationships). The definition of social presence was therefore revised as: "the ability of participants to identify with the community (e.g., course of study), communicate purposefully in a trusting environment, and develop inter-personal relationships by way of projecting their individual personalities" (Garrison 2009, p. 352).

This modest but important revision shifted the initial emphasis from interpersonal relationships to identification with and processes in supporting the creation of a cohesive community of inquiry. This shift was precipitated and supported by research on group identity. Rogers and Lea (2005) argued that it is shared social identity and not personal identity that is essential for a group to coalesce. They suggested that interpersonal bonds and personal goals, in fact, could undermine cohesive group behavior. That is, strong personal relationships could well restrict the open communication that is essential to build cohesion. The issue of participants' implicit collusion to act uncritically and avoid conflict was raised by Kennedy and Kennedy (2010) in the context of communities of inquiry and they noted its risk of undermining group cohesion. They label this non-critical thinking as groupthink and state that "groupthink represents the negative side of group safety, and is a chief inhibitor of inquiry" (Kennedy and Kennedy 2010, p. 12). This is the essence of the argument made previously for thinking collaboratively to mitigate confirmation bias.

The balance of creating a secure climate but not to the degree that it restricts open communication was the motivation behind the shift of emphasis from interpersonal issues in the social presence construct. This re-examination and refinement of the social presence construct was to emphasize the importance of critical discourse and ensure that participants identify with the purpose of the group before establishing interpersonal relationships that could undermine critical thinking. This refinement was to dispel the myth that social presence is first and foremost about socio-emotional issues. Social presence must be seen as being directed to establishing an environment for open communication (discourse) and establishing purposeful group cohesion essential for deep and meaningful learning and academic achievement. This, of course, must include addressing socio-emotional concerns but in the context of attending to purposeful communication issues associated with respect of individuals expressing reasonable contrary views. Purposeful academic identity with the group must be stronger than interpersonal relationships within the group if an environment for critical discourse is to be established and avoidance of personal confirmation bias is to be achieved. Personal and emotional affiliations should be allowed to develop naturally but care must be exercised to ensure personal relationships do not undermine open communication.

The refinement of the social presence construct has been supported in recent research. One such study explored the strength of social ties (commitment, cohesion) using the social presence construct (Kovanovic *et al.* 2014). Beyond the theoretical support for the construct, the study concluded that "students' social presence develops mostly through interactions focused on learning" (Kovanovic *et al.* 2014, conclusion). That is, social presence is developed by engaging students in clearly defined academic expectations and affective expressions did not directly stimulate discussions. The authors also suggest that engaging in the exchange of ideas contributes to developing a sense of community. Similarly, Kozan and Richardson (2014) found that social interactions were used primarily for learning purposes. Thus, it is argued that personal relationships should naturally result as a byproduct of purposeful academic interactions. These findings support the revised social presence construct in that participants identify first with the academic purpose of the group and, at the outset, social presence should be grounded in open academic communication and not directly personal relationships.

There is also evidence that social presence has a strong influence on student achievement and satisfaction, particularly in an online learning environment (Zhan and Mei 2013). However, another revealing study found that social presence is related to student satisfaction but is mediated through cognitive engagement (absorption) (Leong 2011). This again suggests that students are satisfied when social presence is cognitively oriented. Undue emphasis on the socio-emotional and personal relationships can unduly shift the identity and focus from the academic or cognitive goals of the group. In a similar way, it has been shown that a sense of community is strongly associated with a sense of cohesion (Abedin *et al.* 2010), but cohesion is not simply a socio-emotional or personal connection. That is, sense of community goes beyond interpersonal connections. Cohesion is very much associated with identity of purpose, focused discourse and facilitation/direction (teacher presence). It has been argued from a pedagogical and learning perspective that group cohesion should be given greater consideration in a community of inquiry (Amemado 2013).

That said, care must be taken not to diminish the importance of the socio-emotional component. Research has shown that effective groups had greater social sensitivity in the sense of reading the non-verbal cues of their teammates. Surprisingly, it was shown that a group's performance was not necessarily related to having a lot of smart people. Engell *et al.* (2014) demonstrated that "having a lot of smart people in a group did not necessarily make a smart group" (p. 2). Moreover, "groups where a few people dominated the conversation were less collectively intelligent [effective] than those with more equal distribution of conversation turn taking" (p. 2). We speculate that this speaks to open communication and group cohesion. However, what is really interesting and important here, however, is that social sensitivity was also evident whether that is face-to-face or reading between the lines in an online environment (Engell *et al.* 2014). That is, social sensitivity is not only important in face-to-face settings but possible and crucial in online environments. This reinforces the importance of belonging and participating fully in the discourse.

Thinking collaboratively does not happen without intent and a supportive (socially sensitive) environment. Thinking and learning collaboratively demands open and honest communication. At the same time, it is not easy for students to express themselves in critical ways and this can adversely affect collaborative approaches and activities (Lambert and Fisher 2013). In this regard, social presence has been shown to be important in supporting collaboration (So and Brush 2008; Zhao *et al.* 2014) and cognitive presence (Kozan and Richardson 2014). There is risk in engaging others in critical discourse and, as we noted previously, this can be an inhibitor if trust and open channels of communication are not established. Moreover, it appears that a certain level of social sensitivity is required to support group collaboration (inquiry), but if it does not focus on group performance, or does not exceed a certain socio-emotional (social sensitivity) threshold, it will likely hinder critical discourse and inquiry (Caspi and Blau 2008; Engell *et al.* 2014; Janssen *et al.* 2012; Lee 2014).

Social presence is an important but complicated construct. A critical step in coping with this complexity is to keep in mind the primary focus of social presence in a CoI framework – that is its support of cognitive presence. However, an important part of social presence is the social emotional environment and social sensitivity of the group. In this way, it is recognized that the essential function of social presence is to create an environment for thinking and learning collaboratively that is connected to the academic goals and dynamic of inquiry.

Cognitive Presence

The cognitive presence construct may well be the least controversial or confusing construct in the CoI theoretical framework. One reason would appear to be the rich history that forms the foundation of this construct. Cognitive presence is grounded in John Dewey's extensive work on reflective thinking and practical inquiry that reflects the generalization of the scientific method. Not to be too facetious, it is hard to argue with the success of the scientific method. From a thinking collaboratively perspective, the key structural feature of the Practical Inquiry model that operationalizes cognitive presence in the CoI framework is the fusion of the private and shared worlds, or the reflection and discourse dynamics (see Figure 5.2). This fusion of the personal and shared worlds is the distinguishing feature of cognitive presence and the model of practical inquiry. This feature is the justification and means to understand thinking and learning collaboratively.

If social presence is the soul of a community of inquiry, cognitive presence is the heart of a community of inquiry (and to extend the physiological metaphor, teaching presence is the backbone, as we shall see). A key challenge of cognitive presence from an educational perspective is to ensure that students move through the phases of inquiry in a timely manner. Moving discourse through to the integration and resolution phases has been seen as an issue in early research. However, it was realized that this is largely dependent upon the nature of the learning tasks designed to achieve specific outcomes and then facilitating the progression of the discourse toward those goals. This progression as a teaching presence responsibility has been confirmed in recent research based on the design and facilitation of learning tasks for students to exhibit appropriate cognitive presence. (Alavi and Taghizadeh 2013; Bai 2009).

Collaborative inquiry through peer support has been shown to positively influence achievement (Purzer 2011). As noted previously, the preeminent value of collaboration and specifically discourse is reflected in the learning sciences research when it is stated that "the best learning takes place when learners articulate their unformed and still developing understanding, and continue to articulate it throughout the process of learning" (Sawyer 2008, p. 53). This has been confirmed where the crucial role of interaction in critical thinking was demonstrated (Saade *et al.* 2012). This adds to the evidence that a sense of community and deep approaches to learning are dependent upon collaborative inquiry as defined by the cognitive presence construct.

Inquiry based on resolving dilemmas and solving problems engages students and increases cognitive presence (Gorsky *et al.* 2010). The evidence is growing that collaborative inquiry creates a sense of achievement and learning satisfaction and is most relevant to collaborative knowledge-building dynamics (Garrison 2011). The research findings go further in that cognitive presence can predict satisfaction and persistence (Jo *et al.* 2011). This study also reinforces the previously stated position that students in a community of inquiry identify with the academic goals of the group and not necessarily social relationships. The point is that students identify with the academic goals of the community and are satisfied and successful when fully engaged in these tasks and not distracted by other relationships. The practical inquiry process (i.e., cognitive presence) can be concisely described as thinking and learning collaboratively.

Teaching Presence

The essential function of teaching presence in a community of inquiry has been documented in previous research (Garrison 2011). Teaching presence is a multi-dimensional construct (design, facilitation and direction) and, through these responsibilities, it is tasked with maintaining a functional community of inquiry. Moreover, this construct has been the most researched and perhaps the best understood CoI element in terms of its importance. A study looking at course design and preparation concluded it "seems that the nature of the learning task assigned to students is a key factor that determines the level of student engagement … while instructor's guidance and assistance activities have significant impact on students' completing learning tasks" (Ma *et al.*, 2015 p. 32). This is a typical finding and reinforces the central role of teaching presence that begins with instructional design.

A recent study of teaching presence with business students provides some interesting insights with regard to the first dimension of teaching presence – instructional design (Wisneski *et al.* 2015). The study found that "instructors who engage students in the communicative process of learning achieved higher levels of teaching presence" (p. 24). Of particular relevance here, this included sharing the instructional design with students so they could understand the expectations. Parenthetically, this process of increasing awareness by sharing also has important implications for metacognition that will be addressed subsequently. Teaching presence was also enhanced when instructors "take the time to acknowledge the contributions of students through words of encouragement, affirmation, or validation" (pp. 24-25). This, of course, moves us to the facilitation dimension of teaching presence and indicates the indivisibility or constant overlap of the components of teaching presence. Consistent with these findings, a study in the area of corporate education concluded that their findings "indicate that focusing exclusively on a single type of interaction [e.g., learner-teacher; learner-learner] during the design phase … may not be desirable" (Rodriguez and Armellini 2014). The point in both studies is that communication and interaction (i.e., engagement) are core considerations in the design process.

From a broader perspective, teaching presence has also been shown to be largely responsible for social and cognitive presence (Rubin and Fernandes 2013). In support of the central function of teaching presence as the backbone of a community of inquiry, it has been shown that in an online context "attainment of the intended learning outcomes relied more on the teaching presence than on social and cognitive presences" (Szeto 2015, p. 191). The central function of teaching presence is also reinforced with its association with perceived learning and satisfaction (Akyol and Garrison 2008; 2011; Jo *et al.* 2011). Based on an analysis of various theories, Croxton (2014) argues that in online learning "interactivity is an important component of [student] satisfaction and persistence" (2014, p. 314) and student-instructor interaction was primarily responsible. As important as student-student interaction is, prompt feedback from instructors is highly valued, motivational and effective. To add to the distinctiveness and complexity of teaching presence, we must be reminded that teaching presence is a distributed responsibility in that all participants are required to actively engage in it to shape the collaborative thinking and learning experience congruent with their abilities. Again this argues for sharing the intended design and requesting input that develops ownership, awareness and shared responsibility.

An exciting development in the research and practice of learning communities is the increased use of the CoI framework to guide the design and assessment of collaborative learning experiences (the first teaching presence responsibility). In this regard the importance of instructional design and organization has been shown to be associated with students' perceived likelihood of success (Kupczynski *et al.* 2010). Similarly, it has been shown that students value the design elements of clear course requirements and academic responsiveness (Saritas 2008; Sheridan and Kelly 2010). In this regard, there are a number of examples where the CoI framework was adopted as a paradigm for course design. The first systematic attempt at using the CoI framework for course (re)design was reported by Vaughan and Garrison (2006). This was part of an initiative of (re) designing over 50 blended learning courses using the CoI framework as the guide. These courses proved to be well received by faculty and students.

A number of other projects have used the CoI theoretical framework and the accompanying survey instrument to design and assess course development initiatives (Ice *et al.* 2011; Kumar *et al.* 2011; Moore and Shelton 2013). It is important to highlight the important role that the CoI survey plays in shaping the evolving design process. The CoI survey can be used to assess the shared perception of a learning community as well as specific shared perceptions of the presences (Rubin and Fernandes 2013). This supports the view that thinking and learning collaboratively can be built into the design of a course using the CoI framework and the CoI survey instrument can be effective in measuring and strengthening the effectiveness of a community of inquiry. In this context, Swan *et al.* (2014) have successfully used the CoI survey instrument to measure the effectiveness of course implementation and provide direction for course improvements. Most importantly, the results have shown "significant increases in student learning outcomes" (p. 79). Finally, it should be noted that the CoI framework is not exclusive to higher education. It has also been used successfully to (re) develop courses at the secondary school level (Jackson *et al.* 2013).

Another area of application of the CoI framework has been for professional development. The importance of using theory for the purpose of creating professional development communities has been noted by Jones and Meyer (2012). In terms of using the CoI framework for faculty development, it should be noted that Vaughan and Garrison (2006) used the CoI framework to create a community of inquiry for faculty whose goal it was to learn how to create a community of inquiry for their students. This professional development model using the CoI framework to guide faculty in creating their own CoI environments for their students has been replicated by Semingson and White (2012). It is argued that there are distinct advantages for faculty development programs that are based on a process of thinking and learning collaboratively. The reason is there is great risk for faculty to fundamentally redesign their course. However, through the development of community and engaging with others regarding course design challenges, faculty gain confidence that they can do this successfully. In addition to the CoI framework, success has also been achieved using the "community of practice" model in redesigning a professional development course (Cochrane and Narayan 2013). This initiative offered a more informal and flexible approach where participants and facilitators negotiated goals. Regardless of the framework shaping faculty development, it can greatly benefit from theoretical guides and a collaborative approach whether it be a comprehensive framework like the CoI or a more informal community of practice model.

An interesting study that considered issues of design showed that detailed participation guidelines (externally-facilitated regulated learning) and scripted role assignments that include both facilitation and direction (specifically scaffolding) had a positive impact on cognitive presence (Gasevic *et al.* 2015). The other variable that produced a positive impact on cognitive presence was externally-induced motivation through grading. The authors of this study concluded that these design strategies improved metacognition and self-regulation by supporting monitoring and managing/controlling responsibilities. This study was inspired by the Garrison and Cleveland-Innes (2005) study that emphasized the importance of structured discourse and strong leadership; however, the caution is not to be overly structured if the goal is thinking and learning collaboratively. While students value clarity, they must not rely on external regulation (teacher direction) inordinately. Moreover, if the goal is to increase shared metacognition, then that must include both self- and co-regulation in a learning environment that is not overly scripted and that encourages distributed teaching presence.

Teaching presence in a community of inquiry has been a focus of much research. However, work remains to better understand the role of the instructor and how teaching presence impacts student learning. Clarke and Bartholomew (2014) took a practical look at understanding the instructor's participation in asynchronous discussions. The results indicated that the instructors were not very good at directing the discussion and supporting cognitive presence. In essence, the instructors' bias was towards support and not challenging thinking. The message here is that teaching presence does not end with facilitation. The results of this study show that if the discourse is to move to issues of critical thinking and practical inquiry, then teaching presence must exhibit a balance of facilitation and direct instruction (directive input and engagement). The authors state that the results further "the idea that we need all three parts of the CoI framework to be effective but how we employ this framework takes a careful and thoughtful balancing act" (Clarke and Bartholomew 2014, discussion, last sentence). In this regard, the results support the position that an effective community of inquiry must keep the academic goals at the forefront if asynchronous online discussions are to be more than chat rooms. The leadership aspect of teaching presence is crucial – interaction is not enough (Garrison and Cleveland-Innes 2005).

Operational leadership is first challenged by the need to ensure that the discourse remains focused and progresses constructively. This means not being seduced by the quantity of interaction but the quality of discourse. Therefore, at some point we must be prepared to move beyond facilitation and on to more directive modes of teaching presence associated with providing timely feedback in the form of suggestions or specific information to move the discourse forward. While this responsibility may well fall largely to the instructor of record, participants should be encouraged to recognize the need for more direct instruction and offer it as required. In this regard, higher levels of cognitive presence have been associated with teaching presence that included feedback and coaching (Stein *et al.* 2013). Similarly, it has been shown that scaffolding discussion strategies with a heuristic can facilitate cognitive presence and critical thinking (Darabi *et al.* 2011). It should also be kept in mind that definitive instructor input appears to be of a greater need for less academically advanced students (Kupczynski *et al.* 2010).

Another design consideration is associated with disciplinary differences. Arbaugh (2013) explored the nature and emphasis of the presences across "hard" and "soft" disciplines. In essence it was hypothesized that greater emphasis is placed on collaboration and facilitation challenges in the soft or qualitative disciplines, while more direct instructional emphasis is placed on presentation of content in the hard or quantitative disciplines. Moreover, it was suggested that there is likely to be a corresponding drop in social presence in the hard disciplines. In this regard, it was concluded that "academic discipline may moderate perceptions of student learning" (Arbaugh 2013, p. 23). From a design perspective, it would appear that courses in the quantitative disciplines did not focus sufficiently on collaboration and facilitation. It was concluded that the quantitative disciplines such as finance and accounting may benefit from more collaborative approaches and attending to social presence. In short, the implication is that the quantitative disciplines could benefit from increased effectiveness by paying greater attention to collaboration, social presence and the facilitation component of teaching presence. These findings were consistent with disciplinary differences found by He (2013).

Before closing this discussion it is important to highlight not only the importance but also the complexity of teaching presence. The teaching presence indicators reflected in the CoI framework and survey instrument do not account for the full range of roles and responsibilities associated with this important construct (Shea *et al.* 2010). However, teaching presence responsibilities as defined by design, facilitation and direct instruction do play an important function in helping us explore and better understand the complexities of thinking and learning in collaborative environments, whether they be online, blended or face-to-face learning experiences. Theoretical frameworks are essential in considering and incorporating new or evolving constructs. A recent and important development that has implications for teaching presence is the shared metacognition construct that focuses on monitoring and managing collaborative thinking and learning. As we shall see next, the shared metacognition construct is an important refinement of the CoI theoretical framework and consistent with its basic collaborative premise.

Shared Metacognition

Thinking collaboratively reveals our thought processes and encourages us to think about our thinking. In this regard, it has been argued that "All inquiry is self-critical practice …" (Lipman 2003, p. 83). However, increasing the awareness of our thought processes in a collaborative environment is greatly enhanced with an appreciation of the inquiry process. Moreover, to be able to successfully navigate the inquiry process requires a willingness and ability to monitor and manage the intended learning goal, associated knowledge, and designed activities and strategies. Therefore, metacognitive awareness can encourage learners to assume teaching and cognitive presence responsibilities leading to deep and meaningful learning (Weerasinghe et al. 2012). A community of inquiry will grow exponentially when all participants become more metacognitively aware and prepared to assume the responsibility of teaching presence by collaboratively monitoring and managing their thinking and learning process. Effective teaching presence inherently demands metacognitive awareness of the inquiry process.

Shared metacognition is revealed at the intersection of teaching presence and cognitive presence. Conceiving metacognition as the integration of cognitive and teaching presence responsibilities found validation in a recent study in that "metacognitive presence correlated significantly with cognitive presence and students' teaching presence" (Weerasinghe et al. 2012, fifth paragraph, Summary of Results). Weerasinghe et al. (2012) also found that cognitive presence (i.e., inquiry) was enhanced as students became more engaged in metacognitive monitoring activities. This was supported in another study that compared a class with no metacognitive awareness of the inquiry process (i.e., cognitive presence) to one that did have metacognitive awareness of inquiry in terms of critical or higher order thinking outcomes (Bai 2009). It was concluded that awareness of the inquiry process facilitated students' critical thinking and when "the students were aware of what discourse was expected, the responses were structured with intent" (Bai 2009, p. 162). Moreover, it was noted that asynchronous online discourse allowed students time to reflect to formulate their thoughts. This apparent advantage to metacognitively reflect on their thoughts was confirmed in another study that reported deeper reasoning for online discussions when compared with face-to-face discussions (Sins et al. 2011).

Shared metacognition integrates individual and social regulatory processes in collaborative learning contexts. In this regard, Flavell (1979) has argued that metacognition is required to explain and justify one's thinking to self as well as to others. Recent work in the area of shared metacognition has validated a shared metacognition construct embedded within the CoI theoretical framework (Garrison and Akyol 2015). The shared metacognition construct extends individual approaches to learning by integrating complementary self and co-regulation dimensions. In this regard, it has been shown that in collaborative learning groups "co-regulation may have benefits for both the person doing the regulating [self-regulation] and other group members …" (DiDonato 2013, p. 41). If learning is considered to be socially situated, then metacognition can no longer be considered solely a self-regulatory ability. Shared metacognition iterates between personal knowledge construction and shared learning activities to confirm understanding through the two interdependent dimensions of self- and co-regulation of cognition (Garrison and Akyol 2015). Self- and co-regulation each exhibit a monitoring (awareness) and a managing (strategic action) function. This construct explains how metacognition is operationalized in collaborative thinking and learning environments. The CoI framework has been essential to defining shared metacognition as the integration of teaching and cognitive presence.

An interesting finding of the shared metacognition study was that female students reflected higher co-regulation scores compared with those of male students. The significance of this is that it fits with a previous study that found "teams with more women outperformed teams with more men" (Woolley *et al.* 2015, 7th paragraph). This was explained by women being more socially sensitive and participatory and would fit with women demonstrating more co-regulation preferences. A somewhat facetious question might be – are women the secret to high performing groups? Perhaps a better question would be to ask whether women have a greater skill (sensitivity, communicativeness) for thinking and learning collaboratively. While caution must be exercised with regard to gender differences, it is important to recognize the importance of social presence in a community of inquiry and how we can best achieve the presence that will support shared metacognition and productive group collaboration.

The shared metacognitive construct is used to explore and understand teaching and cognitive presence in a collaborative learning environment. An initial validation study of a shared metacognition questionnaire reflecting self and co-regulation has been reported recently (Garrison and Akyol 2015). This questionnaire (see Appendix B) represents an important tool to study a range of metacognitive questions in collaborative learning environments. In addition to further validation of the questionnaire, further study could open opportunities to conduct quantitative studies of mutually supported cognition with larger samples that are not possible with qualitative methodologies. The shared metacognitive construct and questionnaire present significant theoretical and practical opportunities for studying thinking and learning in communities of inquiry. The shared metacognition construct offers considerable potential to further refining the CoI theoretical framework in terms of how the presences interact.

The shared metacognition construct described here begins with an understanding of the practical inquiry process and the integration of reflective and regulatory elements. Participants in a community of inquiry are required to be both learners and teachers – to take responsibility for cognitive and teaching presence. Cognitive presence looks at constructing meaning from the inside-out, while teaching presence looks at the strategic management of inquiry from the outside-in. However, shared metacognition is a fusion of cognitive and teaching presence that does not present a bias toward either internal or external perspectives; both are necessary for thinking and learning collaboratively. Metacognition in a collaborative thinking and learning environment is an integrated self- and co-regulated inquiry process for constructing personal meaning and collaboratively confirming understanding.

Summary

The previous review of research provides insights into the theoretical and practical understanding of collaborative inquiry. Recent research has consistently validated the CoI framework and provided theoretical and practical direction to designing and facilitating thinking and learning in collaborative educational environments. Looking at each of the presences, we see that social presence provides the environment for a collaborative, cohort-based approach to thinking and learning. Social presence has evolved to focus on identification with the academic goals of a learning community. Cognitive presence is the core of a community of inquiry and, as such, focuses on thinking and learning collaboratively. With regard to the third element, teaching presence, research has shown it to be the crucial element in establishing and sustaining a community of inquiry. While teaching presence may be the most researched presence, the complexity and importance of its role does not diminish the need for further research into this element of a community of inquiry. That said, perhaps the most exciting new area of research is that of shared metacognition. The self and co-regulation dimensions of shared metacognition defines the inseparability of cognitive and teaching presence for an inquiry based learning experience.

Thinking collaboratively requires the support of like-minded participants in terms of common goals, an appreciation of meaningful inquiry, and a commitment to other participants. The central idea is to think for one's self but in the context of others so that thinking and learning can be advanced through the sharing and justifying of reasons (Kennedy and Kennedy 2010). The important point is that the individual does not give up their individuality and uniqueness of thought, but has them advanced and confirmed through collaborative inquiry. This has been explored in the study of the CoI framework and understanding the art of balancing social, cognitive and teaching elements.

In conclusion, it is worthwhile to note that while the CoI framework has focused on online and blended learning approaches, its source of inspiration was not in these areas of study and practice. Its philosophical and theoretical foundation has its genesis in traditional higher education and, as such, is generalizable to purposeful learning environments that are committed to collaboratively constructing personal meaning and confirming understanding. The CoI theoretical framework with its embedded principles can be invaluable in designing and supporting collaborative approaches to deep and meaningful learning experiences regardless of context. The CoI framework can help us cope with the theoretical and practical challenges of constructing collaborative thinking and learning transactions. Moreover to realistically monitor and manage thinking and learning collaboratively, the focus must be on a derivative set of principles and not procrustean recipes. Exploring these principles is the focus of the next chapter.

7

PRINCIPLES OF PRACTICE

Nothing is so practical as a good theory.

(Lewin 1945.)

We have argued that thinking collaboratively is best realized through a purposeful and cohesive community of inquiry characterized by free and open communication. However, the complexity of this challenge demands more than recipes or a short list of best practices. There are no quick fixes when it comes to designing collaborative approaches to deep and meaningful thinking and learning. Notwithstanding this design challenge, the Community of Inquiry (CoI) framework has been shown to be effective in providing a parsimonious ordering and understanding of the complexities of thinking and learning collaboratively, and it is a promising guide to designing such learning experiences. The basis of this promise is a set of principles deduced from the CoI theoretical framework that reflects the transactional nature of thinking and learning collaboratively. It is these principles that we explore in this chapter framed by teaching presence and its sub-elements and responsibilities of design, facilitation and direct instruction.

A community of inquiry is a group of individuals engaged in thinking collaboratively through the purposeful and recursive process of reflection and discourse to construct personal meaning and confirm mutual understanding. Coping with the practical challenges of designing and delivering a collaborative thinking and learning experience can be greatly aided by a set of guiding principles. The principles described next were deductively derived from the CoI theoretical framework.

Principles

One of the most consistent findings of research on the CoI framework since its inception is the central role and importance of teaching presence; it is the backbone of a community of inquiry. From a pragmatic perspective we must be reminded that teachING presence (not teachER presence) is a distributive responsibility in that the challenge is to share pedagogical responsibilities among the participants of the learning community. This creates a paradoxical environment in that the instructor "attempts both to exert and not exert control, and teaches by not teaching" (Kennedy and Kennedy 2010, p.12). This recursive process and balancing act is the core dynamic of teaching presence in a community of inquiry.

Recognizing the importance of teaching presence, seven principles of practice have been deduced from the CoI theoretical framework from this perspective. Issues of social and cognitive presence are addressed according to each of the three categories of teaching presence – design, facilitation and direct instruction. As such, there are principles of social and cognitive presence associated with each of the three categories of teaching presence. Assessment is identified as a separate principle considering its generalized importance and influence on how students approach the learning experience.

The seven principles of practice for a CoI (Garrison 2011) are:

1) Plan for the creation of open communication and trust (social presence);
2) Plan for critical reflection and discourse (cognitive presence);
3) Establish community and cohesion (social presence);
4) Establish inquiry dynamics (cognitive presence);
5) Sustain respect and responsibility (social presence);
6) Sustain inquiry that moves to resolution (cognitive presence);
7) Ensure assessment is congruent with intended processes and outcomes.

The first two principles focus on social and cognitive presence issues associated with designing a collaborative thinking and learning experience. Similarly, the next two principles focus on social and cognitive presence concerns associated with facilitating a collaborative thinking and learning experience. The fifth and sixth principles address social and cognitive presence demands associated with the need for direct instruction. Finally, the seventh principle, the ever present assessment influence, pervades all the presences.

Before we go further it is important to emphasize the interdependence of these presences and the reality that any specific strategy will be influenced by more than one principle. We also note the following discussion is focused around supporting reflection and discourse in a technologically rich environment. That is, a blended environment that thoughtfully integrates synchronous and asynchronous verbal, text and graphic communication.

Design

Design is the obvious first step in any purposeful learning experience. The design process guided by a coherent framework will encourage thoughtful decisions regarding the process to achieve the intended learning outcomes. The design process will invariably prove to be more effective and efficient when shaped by a set of principles. It must also be kept in mind that designing collaborative thinking and learning shaped by inquiry is an ongoing process. Design issues will continually present themselves as the needs and interests of the community of inquiry evolve. Notwithstanding the fluid nature of design in a collaborative learning environment, a well thought through design at the outset will provide greater flexibility in adjusting to the evolving needs and interests of the group. Principles embedded in a theoretical framework can provide a systematic approach to optimal design for collaborative thinking and learning.

Social Presence

The first principle of practice associated with thinking collaboratively in a community of inquiry is the need to establish a presence that will support open communication and the development of a cohesive group identity. Social presence mediates between teaching and cognitive presence and has been shown to be associated with perceived learning and persistence (Eom and Arbaugh 2011). In this regard, the primary goal is to create a climate that encourages and supports open communication through a sense of belonging and trust. To begin this process, an effective initial activity would be to have participants post a short biography. While inter-personal relationships will need time to develop, this can be initiated early by sharing some background information through more purposeful academic activities. Clearly, creating social presence is essential if we are to critically explore ideas.

A climate of trust may well be established more quickly in a face-to-face environment but there are several strategies that can be employed in asynchronous online learning environments to enhance engagement and create a sense of community. An effective activity at the outset in either a face-to-face verbal environment or an online text environment is to allow participants in small groups to critically analyze the goals and expectations of the intended learning experience. This will give participants an opportunity to identify with the purpose of the learning community and help clarify expectations while beginning to develop personal relationships. Another consideration is to indicate the importance of engaging in discourse by assigning a nominal grade for participation. With that in mind, it is not recommended that the quality of participation be assessed as this can serve to restrict open communication. The suggestion is to simply assign a pass/fail grade. Through these activities not only can a climate begin to be established but important design elements may be modified at the outset. This will also provide an opportunity to model thinking collaboratively through academically relevant discourse. Examples of other activities that can build social presence in an online environment can be found in Vaughan *et al.* (2013, p. 28) which is an open source publication available online.

Building collaborative and trusting environments has been shown to be a successful strategy that is supported in the literature (deNoyelles *et al.* 2014). Modeling social cues such as using names, providing encouragement and sharing experiences has also proven to enhance the sense of community and group cohesion. In terms of modeling collaborative engagement, another important design consideration is a participation protocol. That is, a clearly delineated set of conditions for engagement describing how often one is expected to contribute, message length, how to respectfully challenge an idea, and when socio-emotional support is appropriate. It has been found that clear directions for engagement promoted "more group cognition and more student ownership of the discussion and empowered students to facilitate themselves ..." (Zydney *et al.* 2012, p. 77). Participants facilitating themselves can also initiate the process of shared metacognition (self- and co-regulation). Discussion etiquette guidelines can be found in Vaughan *et al.* (2013, p. 30). Attending to the conditions for social presence establishes a climate for thinking collaboratively and will influence cognitive presence design strategies.

Cognitive Presence

The second principle of practice for thinking collaboratively in a community of inquiry considers the planning of the learning experience itself.

The first obvious task in planning a learning experience is the selection of subject matter, resources and associated activities. This is a formidable challenge if we are to encourage deep and meaningful approaches to learning and not over-burden learners with content and assignments. As noted previously, prescribing excessive content is one of the main deterrents to approaching collaborative thinking and learning in deep and meaningful ways. It is a barrier to exploring the content through discourse and assimilating the content in deep and meaningful ways. One strategy to address this is to organize content around major themes, which provides the time to focus on nontrivial subject matter. In short, the design task is to provide thoughtfully structured content and the time to discuss and reflect upon the meaning and implications of the ideas presented.

After selecting and organizing the subject matter, the next crucial challenge is the design of discussion prompts and collaborative learning activities. If the goal is to have the learners move through all phases of the inquiry process, then activities must be designed in which it is clear that a resolution is expected. Project assignments are excellent activities that have a clear outcome and collaboratively engage learners throughout the inquiry process. What should be avoided is posting general questions without clear expectations. Another consideration is that opportunity to engage in discourse is shaped by the size of the group. The size of the group matters – too few and you don't get the diversity of thought that can stimulate discourse; too many and you lose the cohesion and opportunity for participation.

As noted previously, assessment influences all aspects of thinking collaboratively and therefore can powerfully shape how learners approach thinking and learning activities. First, formative assessment is very helpful in setting a constructive climate that reinforces participation in a community of inquiry. To reiterate, the best plans to encourage deep approaches to learning can be undermined if assessment is not commensurate with intended learning activities and outcomes. Grading simple recall of information insidiously undermines collaborative thinking associated with constructing deep meaning and understanding. Assimilating information does not require thinking and learning collaboratively and learners will resist or half-heartedly and superficially interact with others. Collaborative projects can be particularly effective in encouraging and assessing deep approaches to thinking collaboratively.

Planning for maximum cognitive presence in a community of inquiry requires an understanding of systematic inquiry that fuses reflection and discourse. This is best accomplished through an understanding of the phases of the inquiry process. When introducing a topic of study, activities should reflect the phases of practical inquiry that include clear expectations and opportunities for exploration, integration and application of ideas for purposes of resolution. Collaboration is of particular importance in the early phases of inquiry, while reflection may predominate during the integration phase. To bring the task to resolution and perhaps application (at least vicariously) may require increased directional support. Finally, it is important to reiterate from a design perspective that adjustments are expected as new ideas and interests emerge.

Facilitation

Facilitation is crucial in creating and sustaining social and cognitive presence. Facilitation is the workhorse in providing support and guidance for thinking and learning collaboratively. In a community of inquiry, facilitation roles and responsibilities are not only open to all participants but being a facilitator is an essential element of the process of thinking and learning collaboratively. It requires that all participants metacognitively monitor and manage the thinking and learning process. In a formal learning environment, however, during the initial stages of the program this is most likely to be the primary responsibility of the instructor. This presents an opportunity to model reflection and discourse while making it clear that participants will be expected to gradually assume increased facilitation responsibilities as an essential component of the inquiry process. Ensuring the appropriate balance between too little or too much facilitation presence by the instructor is an important consideration and crucial to achieve intended levels of cognitive presence.

Social Presence

The third principle, associated with the social dimension of thinking collaboratively, is focused on facilitating group identity and cohesion through open communication. To think collaboratively, participants need to feel comfortable engaging in critical thinking and discourse. As noted previously, the first task is to establish and facilitate an environment for open communication and group cohesion. All participants must be aware of the social climate and take responsibility to facilitate open communication that will build group cohesion. To accomplish this, participants need teaching presence to model the facilitation of discourse that does not undermine continued engagement. Somebody needs to provide the leadership that sets a welcoming tone for the openness that makes participants feel comfortable and responsible to objectively evaluate what they reason to be erroneous ideas or arguments. The key at the outset is to have clear norms and guidelines as to how participants are to engage socially and emotionally with the community to sustain motivation and persistence.

However, the goal is not to make everybody feel emotionally comfortable. This has to be a by-product of a worthwhile and satisfying learning experience. That is, facilitation of social presence is not done in an academic vacuum. Therefore, the focus should not just be on the socio-emotional dimension and interpersonal relationships. To focus excessively on interpersonal relationships is to risk obscuring and undermine the reasons why the participants are there. They are there for a particular academic purpose – to engage in a worthwhile and meaningful collaborative thinking and learning experience. In this regard, the academic interests of the participants must remain at the forefront. As important as developing interpersonal relationships is, they must be allowed to develop naturally through substantive interactions around the cognitive interests and demands of a deep and meaningful learning experience. The challenge is to facilitate the development of social presence through a focus on academic pursuits. Interestingly, if participants feel the academic focus is compromised, they will either resist or withdraw their participation.

While the goals for facilitating social presence in face-to-face or online contexts are similar, specific demands may shift (see Vaughan *et al.* 2013, p. 50 for specific face-to-face and online facilitation strategies). In a face-to-face environment visual cues may be very helpful in engaging with others, while being intimidating for some. On the other hand, in an online environment it may prove more difficult for individuals to get to know each other but more reserved participants may well feel freer to contribute to the discussion. We must consider that face-to-face contact can be an inhibitor of critical discourse. It may be harder to challenge the ideas of individuals with whom we have a close relationship and this is why we must provide guidelines for critical discourse early on. There is some evidence that creating trust in a face-to-face context may be more important and challenging (Bierly *et al.* 2009). Conversely, one might surmise that group cohesion in online contexts is more dependent on task focus and clarity than trust *per se*. Regardless, the key to both of these contexts is to first engage participants in smaller groups and allow them to learn to facilitate their discussions while getting to know each other through academic engagement.

Cognitive Presence

The fourth principle of practice for thinking collaboratively in a community of inquiry is facilitating the inquiry process. As a secure environment has begun to be established, the emphasis shifts to issues of cognitive presence operationalised through the inquiry process. The external manifestation of this process is discourse predicated upon purposeful, open communication. The first level of facilitation is Socratic questioning that causes learners to reflect and then to further guide them with additional questions toward intended learning outcomes. At the second level is more critical questioning to "challenge students to defend their position, play 'devil's advocate' by providing opposing evidence, highlighting different student opinions, or prompting students to consider alternative viewpoints" (deNoyelles *et al.* 2014, p. 159). This segues into more direct instruction to be discussed in the next section. Facilitating cognitive presence should challenge the biases and thinking of the participants while ensuring the intended objectives are achieved in a timely manner. Facilitation requires focusing the discussion, challenging ideas, identifying areas of agreement or disagreement, and creating a summary (see Vaughan *et al.* 2013, p. 55 for other strategies to facilitate cognitive presence). One of the great skills for facilitating cognitive presence is to ask the right questions at the right time such that it precipitates deeper reflection and discourse.

Certainly modeling the facilitation of discourse and critical questioning is crucial if participants are to assume responsibility to construct and confirm meaning through discourse. In this regard, an important activity is for the participants to increase their awareness of the inquiry process itself. That is, collaboratively increasing metacognitive awareness by stepping back and formatively assessing the progression of the thinking and learning experience itself. A study of online discussion forums found "that students take the role of facilitator seriously and use metacognitive processes … but instruction and guidance is needed" (Snyder and Dringus 2014, p. 44). In this regard, facilitative questioning can be instrumental in increasing metacognitive awareness and assuming greater cognitive presence by collaboratively guiding participants in such discussions. Moreover, in a collaborative thinking and learning experience this should not be left entirely to the instructor. Developing metacognitive awareness collaboratively through an understanding of the phases of inquiry is essential for continued learning effectiveness. Enhancing the participants' metacognitive awareness of the inquiry process may well be the most effective means of facilitating thinking and learning collaboratively.

"Devil's Advocate" [handwritten marginal note]

An effective way for participants to appreciate metacognitive awareness and co-regulation of the learning experience is to have the participants moderate a discussion. Here participants learn the art of facilitating discussion in terms of knowing when to intervene, when to move the discussion along, and when to summarize achievements. It has been shown that peer facilitation can increase engagement and cognitive presence (deNoyelles *et al.* 2014). Peer facilitators are less intimidating and therefore have an advantage to draw in participants. In this regard it is interesting to note that worry had an adverse effect on metacognition (Massoni 2014). However, while peer facilitation can be significant, the challenge for the instructor is knowing when to intervene. A recent study has provided a model that classifies students' expectations of facilitator intervention that can be useful in helping an instructor to know when to be actively involved (Sherratt 2012). The goal is to create the conditions (both security and knowledge) that breed confidence for learners to fully engage in critical discourse and assume responsibility to monitor and manage their learning.

Participants need to reflect upon and share their metacognitive awareness during a collaborative assignment by thinking collaboratively about thinking collaboratively. A clear metacognitive understanding of the dynamics of inquiry will prepare learners to collaboratively shape their thinking. However, there are times where more expertise is required to direct the inquiry and provide specific content. Regardless of who is facilitating, it must be recognized that too much facilitation can stifle discourse as well as too little. A guideline for student moderated discussions can be found in Vaughan *et al.* (2013, p. 77). Another important activity for metacognitive awareness would be to have students debrief a collaborative assignment by describing the approach, identifying challenges at the time, and what was learned in terms of strategies. This activity is likely to open the transaction to more directive teaching presence responses.

Direct Instruction

At first glance direct instruction may seem somewhat antithetical to thinking and learning collaboratively. However, teaching presence in a community of inquiry is much more than a guide on the side. Structure and leadership are assets, not constraints, in a purposeful learning experience. To be clear, direction is as much a shared responsibility as facilitation. Direct intervention moves beyond facilitation in terms of rigor and productivity. Interestingly, direct instruction becomes more prevalent in the inquiry process as the group approaches the resolution phase. Timely leadership is welcomed in a collaborative thinking and learning context to provide direction and feedback. In thinking and learning collaboratively, there is the expectation that others can constructively provide timely input in terms of maintaining the appropriate climate, providing new information, diagnosing misconceptions, or metacognitively regulating the discourse. These are examples of direct instructional input.

Social Presence

The fifth principle of practice for thinking and learning collaboratively is to sustain interpersonal respect and responsibility. The task of direct instruction in terms of social presence is to maintain the academic climate. That is, sustaining an environment that continues to value open communication and group cohesion such that assumptions and questionable ideas can be challenged.

An example where direct social presence intervention is required is when insensitive personal comments are made that may damage open communication. Social presence intervention may also be required when the discussion gets overly heated or personally critical. Interestingly, this is more common an occurrence in online discussions. The opposite is often the case in face-to-face environments; that is, being overly polite and not willing to challenge misconceptions. In both contexts it is essential that the right balance of respect and academic integrity be struck. Participants must not feel they are being attacked personally. It is a real challenge to be clear that ideas and not individuals are being challenged; or, conversely, that important but difficult issues are not ignored due to misplaced politeness or an unwillingness to challenge personal biases. Opportunities to discuss the social climate for inquiry should be provided through direct instruction.

Positive motivation is the result of concurrently attending to all of the CoI presences. Social presence plays a critical role in mitigating natural fears associated with collaborative approaches to thinking and learning. Sustaining a secure but curious thinking and learning climate enhances the satisfaction and joy of an engaged learning experience. These emotional states are outcomes of a successful learning experience that then reinforces motivation and a sustained effort. That said, awareness and explicit attention must be directed to frustrations that inevitably arise in a collaborative learning environment if we are to manage motivational states.

Cognitive Presence

The sixth principle of practice for thinking and learning collaboratively is to sustain inquiry through reflection and discourse such that intended goals are achieved. Direct instruction from a cognitive perspective ensures that participants achieve their learning goals in a timely manner. It must be anticipated that progression through the phases of inquiry may be stalled and direction will be required to productively move things forward. This will mean providing explicit leadership in terms of focusing on the key concepts, providing information when needed, shifting direction according to academic needs, intervening to address misconceptions, moving the process to resolution, and providing discussion summaries. Discussion summaries should minimally include key issues identified, conclusions drawn, how lessons could be applied, and what are the key resources. Thinking collaboratively requires that all participants actively contribute to this process using direct intervention when necessary.

Participants must be prepared to offer ideas of how to achieve intended outcomes. Direct instructional skills can be developed and distributed through discourse protocols, modeling direction, moderating discourse, and providing cogent summaries of the learning experience from both a process and content perspective. This progression of activities provides a means to develop metacognitive awareness and strategies to sustain a worthwhile collaborative thinking and learning experience. As with facilitation, an important caveat is that a delicate balance must be struck with regard to direction. Too much or too little direction will adversely impact the engagement of the participants and their willingness to assume teaching presence responsibilities. Direction includes a strong evaluative component that must be shared and defended.

Assessment

The seventh principle for thinking and learning collaboratively is to ensure assessment is congruent with intended processes and outcomes. As has been stated, how learning is measured and rewarded will overwhelmingly shape the approach to learning and ultimately the quality of learning outcomes. Formative assessment is the first and perhaps most important challenge in thinking and learning collaboratively. The question is the nature of the feedback that will support deep and meaningful approaches to collaborative thinking and learning. Constructive feedback should include ideas to consider, ways to improve discourse, motivational encouragement, and awareness of progression to intended outcomes.

Assessment is overarching and demands that all presences be considered when offering constructive feedback. While the substance of the feedback may well address cognitive presence issues, teaching and social presence issues must also be considered. For example, when engaged in discourse (cognitive presence), what might be the best way to explain a misconception (teaching presence); and what contextual or affective issues (social presence) need to be addressed to ensure the individual remains committed to the task and connected to the group. Moreover, all participants must assume responsibility for constructive formative feedback and for ensuring the integration of all the presences for the support of thinking and learning collaboratively. It is critically important that feedback is not only provided by the instructor of record. This will very quickly risk shutting down collaborative inquiry.

Formal learning environments are also shaped by the reality of assigning grades. Much of what is accomplished through sound formative feedback can be undone by judgmental summative assessment that is not congruent with the activities and goal of deep and meaningful learning outcomes. Moreover, deep approaches to learning associated with thinking collaboratively will be undermined or lost if the grade assessment is based on simple recall. It is important that the participants are clear about how they are going to be assessed through the use of assessment rubrics and that assessment reflects deep and meaningful learning. Good examples of assessment rubrics can be found in Vaughan *et al.* (2013). Evidence of thinking collaboratively can be gained through online discussion forums or collaborative assignments that require individual contributions to a shared document. Individual written assignments can also include a collaborative component by sharing drafts of the manuscript and getting feedback to help shape the document.

Finally, metacognitive awareness is also an important element of both formative and summative assessment. Consideration needs to be given to assessing the effectiveness of the process itself. The effectiveness of thinking and learning collaboratively must include reflective feedback about how the inquiry process could be improved. Assessment of the process is as important as achieving intended learning outcomes. If the process itself is not effective the quality of the results are bound to be questionable.

Summary

The CoI theoretical framework speaks directly to how we create and sustain purposeful learning communities. While we have explored a set of specific principles associated with each of the elements of a community of inquiry for purposes of thinking and learning collaboratively, we must keep in mind that any derivative strategy or technique may have a direct impact on one presence but will inevitably impact the other presences. It is the interaction of the presences in concert that creates and sustains an effective community of inquiry. This suggests a complexity with regard to thinking and learning collaboratively that must be addressed. It is the Community of Inquiry framework that provides the order and rationale to manage this complexity. This framework offers a comprehensive approach to creating and sustaining a community of learners engaged in thinking and learning collaboratively.

Beyond the core internal dynamics of a community of inquiry there are exogenous variables that also must be considered if we are to support and sustain thinking and learning collaboratively. Examples include communication technology options, disciplinary demands, and the level and ability of the participants. Such considerations raise larger organizational issues. Educational institutions have traditions and structural realities that inherently enhance or constrain possibilities for thinking and learning collaboratively. As a result, it is the issue of institutional leadership, essential to create and sustain collaborative approaches to thinking and learning, that we turn to next.

8

LEADING COLLABORATIVELY

... more and more, people are beginning to view leadership as a way of working with others in a group rather than a set of personality traits that an individual needs to gain a position of authority.

(Kathleen Allen 2004.)

New ways of thinking about leadership are challenging hierarchical leadership structures that are neither effective nor sustainable. We do not see leadership as the mythical charismatic individual who we have traditionally seen as the typical if not ideal leader of an organization. The essential argument here is that leadership must engage individuals across an organization for significant change to be successful. This is a process of leading collaboratively to understand the nature of organizational change and innovation. What is becoming increasingly apparent is that thinking collaboratively is required to solve complex organizational problems and to lead in disruptive times.

Collaborative approaches to thinking and learning have distinct advantages when confronting organizational change. It improves the possibility of bringing forward diverse perspectives and ideas essential for growth. Perhaps, more importantly, it creates the conditions to challenge basic assumptions essential for the transformation of an organization. In the context of organizational leadership, Argyris (1976; 1977) describes double-loop learning as a process where basic assumptions are challenged through discourse. Double-loop learning creates learning environments where participants enhance their opportunities for learning through shared control. This is in essence creating a community of inquiry at an organizational level. It is a process of inquiry that takes leaders beyond simply questioning tactics and into the realm of questioning basic assumptions. Leading collaboratively is transformational and dependent upon thinking and learning collaboratively.

Leading collaboratively creates an organizational culture where leadership is a shared responsibility. It is a culture where open communication creates the cohesion to address difficult organizational challenges. Conditions are created for dialogue and debate where complex issues can be raised and considered. The principles of a community of inquiry can be directed to creating a culture of leading collaboratively. From an organizational perspective the principles of a community of inquiry remain the same, only the bureaucratic and hierarchical nature of the challenges are diffused. Purposeful commitment, open communication and group cohesion are essential elements when collaboratively inquiring into organizational challenges, change and innovation. Collaborative inquiry necessitates that leaders invest in the culture of the organization that reflects a climate of trust, shared responsibility and clear direction. This is a community culture where participants are encouraged to exercise leadership and it is the hallmark of successful organizations (Rohman 2014b).

Collaboration and Bureaucracy

Not unlike a community of inquiry, the culture of successful organizations has to be a climate of free and open communication. It is hard to argue with the central role that open communication has in thinking, learning and leadership. However, thinking collaboratively for leadership is more than exchanging information. From an organizational perspective this point is made by Schrage (1995) when he states:

> Organizations that attempt to substitute increased communications for increased collaboration will learn the hard way that there is a tremendous difference. Flooding someone with more information doesn't necessarily make him a better thinker (p. 5).

The communication technologies that surround us greatly influence how we think and solve problems but these technologies must be predicated on more than simply providing access to information. Communication technologies must support transactions where participants are able to share ideas and be included in making decisions. Participants must be empowered to identify problems and find potential solutions. Collaborative leadership is the recognition that senior leaders cannot possibly be everywhere and make all the decisions (Rohman 2014b). The bottom line is that technology can bring people together but it does not necessarily mean more meaningful thinking and discourse. Technology will be of little help if there is not a culture of thinking and leading collaboratively.

Collaboration in thinking and leading demands a purposeful and shared inquiry into important and challenging problems. From an organizational perspective, leadership demands that individuals see themselves as an integral part of a team, not individuals with separate tasks that demand only that they cooperate and not be an impediment. There is an important difference between cooperation and collaboration. Cooperation in an organization too often means that you just do your job and don't worry about the bigger picture. Collaboration, on the other hand, is working with others on common problems. Effective groups are distinguished by "members who communicated a lot, participated equally and possessed good emotion-reading skills" (Woolley *et al.* 2015, 3rd last paragraph). In this sense, leading collaboratively is about purposeful engagement with others across all levels of an organization and across various interest groups. This raises the challenge of having participants consider the larger organizational goals while concurrently weighing the impact on their particular responsibilities and contributions. For this reason, it is argued that the greatest barrier to collaborative leadership is excessive levels of bureaucracy.

Bureaucracies result in a diffusion of purpose, building empires and hiding incompetence. This is the antithesis of collaborative leadership. As bureaucracy grows, the more isolated the leadership becomes and it is progressively unable to recognize and deal with impending challenges. Higher education institutions have not moved in the direction of most other organizations in terms of flattening their organizational structure. Universities have been expanding their administration and support personnel with the result that "institutions of higher education are mainly controlled by administrators and staffers who make the rules and set more of the priorities of academic life" (Ginsberg 2011, p. 1). Moreover, Ginsberg states: "Administrators and staffers actually outnumber full-time faculty members at American colleges and universities" (p. 24). This is in contrast to a time four decades previously when faculty far outnumbered administrators. Sadly, "the faculty to student ratio has remained fairly constant over the past thirty years" (Ginsberg 2011, p. 26) while the administrative bureaucracy continues to grow.

An illustrative example of the growth of the administrative bureaucracy in higher education is from a long-time department head. He described how his responsibilities "evolved from that of a faculty member with some administrative duties to one in which we must be budget and efficiency experts, time management specialists, and politically savvy academicians" (Pinto 2014, p. 17). Moreover, Pinto states that the performance evaluations associated with the large list of administrative duties have "taken on disproportionate importance to the basics of teaching well and effectively and maintaining a good dose of active and engaged learning in our classrooms" (p. 17). From here he asks the crucial question: "How does the chair of 2014 maintain excellence in teaching, satisfy the need for a diligent and effective administrator and recruiter, and lead the faculty academically through a greatly volatile time in higher education?" (p. 17). This is the key question and dilemma facing leaders in higher education. How do leaders focus on the core mandate of teaching and learning in an overwhelming bureaucratic organization that represents a diversion from pedagogic and technological developments in thinking and learning?

Bureaucratization of educational institutions with their public and academic mission makes little sense. Academic inquiry is founded on open communication free from management regulation. Bureaucracies isolate individuals and undermine constructive relationships. What then is the purpose of expanding the managerial bureaucracy whose values and activities are often quite removed from the collegial culture of academic inquiry? Nearly a century ago John Dewey cautioned about "the undue importance given to administrative activities, which then encroach upon the time and energy which should go to study and teaching" (cited in Martinez-Aleman 2012, p. 83). Unfortunately, the administrative bureaucracy has grown dramatically at the same time that significant administrative and technological demands have been shifted down to faculty. The result, predicted by Dewey, is the emphasis on the "conspicuous activity" of the administrative bureaucracy at the expense of research and teaching.

In this scenario, it is not hard to see that management risks becoming more disconnected from the academic concerns of faculty and students. While faculty control the academic content and dynamics in the classroom, the operation of the institution is conducted in relative isolation from faculty and often serving the narrow interests of bureaucrats. The reality is that collaborative thinking and learning are not the primary concern of senior management in higher education. Yes, senior management do give lip service to improving the quality of the learning experience but spend most of their time with budgets, fund development and ceremonial duties. The associated risk is with mid-level administrators that too often are more concerned with developing fashionable services and growing mini-empires. This result is a diversion of resources and the creation of more administrative units that do not directly serve students and faculty.

Another bureaucratic diversion is the susceptibility to reinventing the wheel. This occurs when new presidents, deans and directors feel impelled to put their brand on the operation by abandoning previous initiatives. An interesting and personal example of this is the decision of one dean to disband departments. As a result, decision making was concentrated through a number of vice and associate deans (interestingly the number of administrators did not decrease). Notwithstanding reduced academic cohesion and opportunity for collaborative leadership, the effect was increased isolation and reduced support for administrative decisions made without adequate consultation. It was increasingly difficult to connect with colleagues on academic matters. Communication, cohesion and morale suffered. It was also more difficult to find the right person to solve an administrative or technical problem. While experienced faculty were able to cope, new faculty struggled.

Whether growth in administrative bureaucracy is defensible or not, the reality is a lack of meaningful strategic collaboration. Administrative growth and the inevitable disconnect with academic goals creates a serious organizational challenge. Opportunities for scholarly communication and collaboration are diminished and the ability of faculty to identify with the goals of the administration is inhibited. Without a commitment to collaboration, individuals become disillusioned and withdrawn. The challenge is to create and sustain collaborative thinking and leading. Significant systemic change will depend on the collaborative efforts of those most closely connected to the core responsibilities of the organization. Without collaborative leadership efforts, change will be isolated, random and inevitably have little lasting impact on the organization.

Sadly, we have too many leaders who are motivated more by ego and celebrity than purpose. Too many are more concerned about building new edifices than they are investing in enhancing the educational experience. We have too many individuals in positions of authority who do not have the vision or courage to take needed positions with regard to the quality of the learning experience. Many times they build buildings in the place of developing sound programs to be seen as doing something; but little changes. Leading collaboratively is not taking the easy path of popular opinion. It is taking the path that addresses important but difficult problems associated with thinking and learning by building understanding through dialogue. It is not the path of perfect. No leader is omniscient or knows exactly what is required. The only path for leadership is to collaboratively engage others in addressing important problems, setting direction and then correcting course as issues emerge. This is the means for sustaining worthwhile change and innovation.

Initiating and Sustaining Change

Innovation in the area of the learning experience is increasingly focused on blending face-to-face and online learning. While blended learning course redesigns are becoming commonplace in higher education, few are grounded in a strategic institutional initiative with the policy and financial support from senior administration. Too often it is seen as one-off course projects associated with unwanted technology innovation. For this reason, it is clear that transformational change must be framed as an institutional strategy with visible leadership from the top. Two cases of institutional change and leadership and the challenges that come with transformational change have been documented (Garrison and Vaughan 2013). In particular it demands "clear organizational plans, strong leadership, and sustained commitment" (Porter *et al.* 2014, p. 24). Clearly this is a strategy of leading collaboratively. All must be on board for major change to be sustained and therefore successful.

Sustaining strategic initiatives is a weak link in successful organizational change and innovation. Speaking from personal experience, I have been in senior leadership positions in two major research universities. My last appointment was to lead an institutional teaching and learning unit. In addition to broad professional development, the institution had adopted a strategic initiative to enhance engagement through blended approaches to teaching and learning. After conducting considerable research and public presentations from international experts on teaching and learning innovation, senior administration endorsed a blended learning course (re)design initiative. At its core was the adoption of instructional designs to engage students in deep approaches to learning using online (asynchronous) and face-to-face (synchronous) approaches where the strengths of online and face-to-face matched particular instructional goals.

The argument offered to faculty was the congruence of blended approaches with the traditions and values of the institution to engage learners in meaningful discourse. For senior administrators it was also noted that blended learning could enhance the learning experience in a cost-effective manner by better utilizing classroom space. These ideas initiated a discussion at all levels of the organization in terms of rethinking how we should approach teaching and learning. We invited faculty to (re)design learning experiences that integrated spontaneous verbal discourse with reflective written communication. The ultimate goal was to facilitate critical, collaborative thinking by creating sustained communities of inquiry – arguably the hallmark of higher education.

The premise was that clear policy positions and action plans are required for change to occur in a desirable and systematic manner and to avoid flavor-of-the-month adoption of new technologies and teaching techniques. Policies were debated and adopted to provide the rationale and gain the support for change across the institution. The approved policy framework presented the case for change through a vision, guiding principles, a rationale, goals, and expected outcomes. However, as important as a vision may be, the real challenge was implementing and sustaining the action plan. A strategic action plan outlined specific initiatives, roles, infrastructure, resources, incentives, professional development, assessment, and accountability measures. The goal was to avoid a well-articulated but inert vision (all too common in educational organizations). Unfortunately, while the vision and policy were approved, the strategic action plan was not formally approved. This proved to be the Achilles heel as leaders from across the institution were not given the opportunity to collaboratively construct and commit to a strategic action plan. As a result, the strategic practical goals and benefits were not kept front and center in a way that would help sustain the initiative. More specifically, without a clear and specific action plan, it was harder to maintain the visibility and essential advocacy from senior leaders. Notwithstanding that over 50 courses in four years were successfully redesigned, not having an official action plan provided an out for the deans.

Funding was inevitably used as an excuse notwithstanding that considerable progress was made with limited resources. The reality was that the deans were not visible partners in raising awareness and generating support. Ultimately this was the undoing of the initiative. The conclusion is that we failed to lead collaboratively. Transformational change in teaching and learning remains elusive in higher education largely due to the enormous challenges of bringing senior leaders onside. It is too easy to agree to a vision and nice sounding words. Academics are very good at that. However, it is another level of difficulty, but critically important, to get senior leaders to committed to specific strategic action plans. This is the challenge of leading collaboratively.

Faculty Development

The faculty culture in higher education is experiencing an erosion of collaboration and community. For significant change in the area of teaching and learning, faculty must be supported in working collaboratively as trusted colleagues. Faculty must be provided with the incentive, support and resources to grow as teaching and learning professionals. Beyond understanding the necessity and benefits for change, the most significant support that can be offered to faculty is constructing community and a collaborative approach to their development. In contrast to the general eroding of collegiality and community in higher education, there are good examples of leading and learning collaboratively in the area of faculty development. These faculty development programs are not just talking about thinking and learning collaboratively, they are designed to model collaborative thinking and learning where faculty experience a community of inquiry. Moreover, the level of collaborative leadership is further enhanced with the inclusion of students in these communities. Students who are continuously engaged through technology can add a much-needed voice in demanding a more thoughtful and engaged learning experience.

Communities are being created where faculty can support each other in collaboratively inquiring into course redesign. It has been shown that faculty want to pursue teaching and learning development in communities where collaboration is respected and there are sustained opportunities to discuss new approaches and ideas (Vaughan and Garrison 2006). Unfortunately, when faculty attend traditional workshops they often lack the opportunity to share their thoughts or receive continuing support in thinking through significant course redesigns. However, the Community of Inquiry framework has been shown to be remarkably successful in creating and sustaining collaboration for designing and delivering courses in higher education (Goldstein *et al.* 2013; Matthews *et al.* 2013; Vaughan and Garrison 2006). This certainly argues for an approach that brings faculty together in a trusting and open environment to experience collaborative approaches to thinking and learning. This collaborative approach to faculty development will be enormously useful as they design these same kinds of thinking and learning experiences for their students.

Teaching development is a complex challenge that requires sustained collaborative support. There is growing evidence that creating a community of inquiry for faculty development will have a significant influence on transforming teaching and learning in higher education. There is a concomitant shift to what happens to students in terms of actively engaging them in the learning process. The success of a faculty development community in support of this shift is dependent upon participants assuming collaborative leadership of the process in terms of discussing new approaches and exploring how they can be made relevant to their context. However, faculty are notoriously private with regard to their teaching and feel vulnerable revealing what transpires in their classrooms. A secure environment must be created before faculty will openly share their thoughts and invite constructive comments. Only in this way will faculty be provided with the direction and ongoing support to implement their course redesigns. In addition, faculty should be provided with the leadership experiences to influence others in terms of developing a culture of thinking and learning collaboratively at the professional level and in the classroom.

Most professions work in teams so why do educators resist? Is it purely financial or a fear of the complexity of learning in a collaborative environment? The reality is that there would be less stress and greater success while extending careers if we could learn to work collaboratively in designing and delivering educational experiences. From a practical perspective it has been shown that to promote professional development leadership is essential, and both face-to-face and online communication complement each other and are indispensable to enhance collaboration among participants (Lin *et al.* 2014). Faculty development that models thinking and learning collaboratively, and that can be sustained over time and distance, may well be the most significant development in bringing faculty onboard in terms of shifting the educational paradigm to collaborative constructivist approaches. Speaking from experience I can attest to how much more enjoyable and rewarding working collaboratively is for all participants in the educational enterprise.

From a broader perspective, collaborative approaches to faculty development build collegial relationships and set examples that can create a better working environment. Participants in faculty development communities have the experience and skills to collaboratively lead course design and delivery in their respective faculties. These then provide examples of leading collaboratively and of ways in which they might be used in other areas of the institution. These faculty development examples can create a culture for thinking and leading collaboratively and encourage others to take responsibility for leading collaboratively. Ultimately, however, senior administration must be open to creating a shared vision and culture for thinking and learning collaboratively. This, of course, will be an arduous and long term challenge in our increasingly bureaucratic educational institutions.

Summary

Thinking collaboratively demands the creation and integration of social, cognitive and teaching presence among the participants. We have argued that leadership is crucial to getting the right balance among these elements. This is true whether it is in the classroom or boardroom. Leadership at the organizational level should be defined as a transactional relationship among various levels of an organization where participants can collaboratively inquire into organizational challenges. Members should be able to identify with the goals of the organization and feel they are part of the decision-making process. This is the essence of community and of thinking collaboratively at the organizational level. The process is no different from those thinking collaboratively about an academic problem in the classroom. Collaborative leadership provides the environment and process where "authority and freedom are in organic union" (Martinez–Aleman 2012, p. 110) – a union where thinking and leading collaboratively can flourish.

9

CONCLUSION

> ... researchers point out that the primary and crucial difference between human cognition and that of other animal species ... is the ability to collaborate for the purpose of achieving shared goals and intentions.
>
> (Wilson 2012, p. 226.)

We have argued that thinking collaboratively is congruent with human nature and appropriate for a connected knowledge society. Meaningful thinking and learning in a knowledge society goes beyond personal reflection and digital literacy. That is, being able to operate a computer or smart phone and staying connected through Twitter says little about critical thinking, knowledge construction and innovation. The realities of living in a connected society require a competency and understanding of the dynamics of meaningful thinking and learning in an unpredictable world. Interactivity has been pushed to the fore with the development of the Internet and social media. However, as we have experienced with social media, interactivity does not necessarily equate with deep thinking and knowledge development.

Thinking collaboratively is a search for community, not simply connection. It is a sense of shared purpose and a collaborative approach to constructing meaning and understanding. To think collaboratively is to invite others into the group to add value to shared deliberations. Community may be enhanced through connective affordances but thinking collaboratively in a community of inquiry represents another dimension beyond simply connecting with individuals. Community provides the conditions to add value to collaborative inquiry. This could include asking probing questions, offering an insight, or providing strategic direction to the discourse. The relevance and timing of the contribution is of prime importance. Communities of inquiry provide the cohesion to sustain critical discourse for reframing experiences and ideas central to approaching mutual understanding.

The ability to collaborate is linked to the origin of human intelligence and evolution (Wilson 2012). Humans have an innate ability to share their thoughts through communication that allows the group to accomplish more than the individual alone. The argument for thinking collaboratively is ultimately grounded in this genetic and cultural heritage. This advantage is operationalized through communication and cohesion within the group. These are the same characteristics that create the environment for a community of inquiry. What has been offered in previous chapters is a framework to help us understand the evolutionary advantages of thinking collaboratively and its relevance in a modern knowledge and technologically connected society. Thinking collaboratively in a community of inquiry provides the balanced tension between individual thoughts and input from the group. At the extremes, the risks that need to be managed in thinking critically are confirmation bias on the part of the individual and conformity and indoctrination from the group. That is, the goals of the individual must be open to the possibility they may be wrong or, on the other hand, the group must not be so focused as to restrict critical exploration. Both individual certainty and group pressure to conform are major barriers to thinking collaboratively. The antidote is creating a dynamic community of inquiry for thinking and learning collaboratively.

Stepping back, it is important to note that the genesis and catalyst in this quest to explore thinking collaboratively was our recent work on shared metacognition (Garrison and Akyol 2015). It was recognized that metacognition is congruent with needing "to communicate, explain, and justify" one's thinking and that "these activities clearly require metacognition" (Flavell 1987, p. 27). Shared metacognition that includes self- and co-regulation constructs was developed to more deeply understand the dynamic of thinking collaboratively – of unifying the personal and shared worlds of thinking and learning collaboratively. The context in which the shared metacognition construct was conceived is the Community of Inquiry framework. The reason for this is that the framework describes the intersection of teaching and cognitive presence, the two constituting dimensions of metacognition, in an environment of collaborative inquiry.

However, before thinking collaboratively can flourish, it must establish a social foundation that goes beyond interpersonal relationships. It requires an identity with the community as well as a secure environment for meaningful discourse. There must be a bond with others in the group if members of the group will feel open to taking the risk to share ideas and expose the viability of one's thinking. Social presence not only provides the foundation for thinking and learning collaboratively, it is also a strong motivational source. Community provides the social environment of cohesion and open communication that allows members to get beyond surface connections and provide the support for members to fully engage in more complex and meaningful intellectual inquiry. Thinking collaboratively cannot be reduced to individual rationality or simplistic activities. It must be recognized that deep and meaningful learning is challenging and demands the concerted consideration of social, cognitive and teaching elements. Thinking and learning collaboratively is inherently a complex process that is further complicated but potentially enhanced by new and emerging communication technologies.

As prevalent and important as communication technologies are, thinking collaboratively must not be defined by the technology, regardless of how beneficial it is in connecting people. We must recognize that it is not the technology that should define how we approach thinking and learning. This must be dependent upon the approach to thinking and learning and secondarily on the nature of the communication required to achieve intended goals – regardless of whether it is face-to-face or online; synchronous or asynchronous. Not having the ideal mode of communication need not fundamentally alter the appropriate approach to thinking and learning. Technology can create a shared space but it should not determine the nature of the thinking and learning transaction. It is the nature of the collaboration that will stimulate thinking and shape the discourse leading to meaningful construction and confirmation of knowledge. The great strength of blended approaches to thinking collaboratively is that the approach is not dependent upon one mode of communication or technology.

Another consideration of communication technologies is the place for face-to-face learning experiences. In terms of thinking collaboratively we have argued for the possibilities of a thoughtful blend of face-to-face and online synchronous and asynchronous learning opportunities. The reason for this is the great benefit of integrating the lively give and take of face-to-face verbal discourse and the reflective engagement made possible by asynchronous written communication. Advances in information and communication technologies should not necessarily be viewed as desirable replacements for learning in face-to-face environments. While face-to-face discourse may not be possible, the option of face-to-face verbal discourse should be very carefully considered and not simply replaced because of technological advances and financial exigencies. Technology does not replace teaching presence whether it is in face-to-face or online learning environments.

It has always been the case that technology has outraced pedagogy. Historically, adoption of learning technologies has been slow and limited in education. However, educational institutions are no longer in the privileged position where they can ignore new and emerging communication technologies as they have become ingrained with engaged approaches to thinking and learning. Generally speaking, we have an analogue pedagogical practice in a rapidly evolving digital world. It is beyond time that we begin to take advantage of the connectivity of the digital world around us to support the evolutionary advantages of collaborative thinking and learning experiences. At the same time, however, it is important to appreciate that simple connectivity is no guarantee of thoughtful collaboration. While new and emerging communication technologies may provide any number of possibilities, the focus must remain on worthwhile and meaningful collaborative inquiry. As a result of technological advances we will see widescale adoption of blended approaches to learning and we can only hope that these developments proceed thoughtfully and with a clear understanding of thinking and learning collaboratively. The issue goes beyond access. We must ask – access to what? It is more than a question of cost; it must be access to a quality learning experience.

Technology and the focus on access was the impetus behind the recent interest in massive open online courses (MOOCs). However, many are questioning the purpose and effectiveness behind these initiatives. A similar skepticism is also being exhibited in the educational use of social media in formal learning contexts. The association between students' social and entertainment use of technology and its use for learning raises the question as to whether students' everyday skills with emerging technologies will correspond to a quality learning experience shaped in a community of inquiry. The transfer from a social or entertainment technology (a living technology) to a learning technology is neither automatic nor guaranteed (Kennedy *et al.* 2008). The fundamental conclusion is that social media inherently provide little opportunity for open communication and dissenting opinions; nor does it provide for and encourage development of leadership in a community of inquiry.

Realization of thinking and learning collaboratively is very much dependent on leadership. This is no different in terms of the classroom or institution. Leaders in any community must be learners and the best leaders are those who can think and learn collaboratively. The best leaders are those who are able to collaboratively reflect on the challenges of the community and then have the courage to make the necessary decisions. Initial decisions, however, do not end the leadership process. The effect of any decision needs to be collaboratively calibrated and adjustments made in a continuous manner. This is no different in the classroom or boardroom. Leadership is a driving and guiding responsibility. The key is always to make that initial decision with as much knowledge as possible but not become catatonic with just one more study or meeting.

This leadership dynamic is the same recursive and collaborative inquiry process that we advocate to overcome confirmation bias – the tendency to see what we want to see – whether it be the classroom or boardroom. Thinking collaboratively is particularly challenging for any leader but particularly so for leaders in senior management positions who often make the mistake of feeling they must have all the answers. The first step is to admit to uncertainty and engage in thinking, learning and leading collaboratively. A community of inquiry at any level of an organization means that we must all think and learn collaboratively as we search for truth.

APPENDIX A

Community of Inquiry Survey Instrument

Teaching Presence

Design and Organization

1. The instructor clearly communicated important course topics.
2. The instructor clearly communicated important course goals.
3. The instructor provided clear instructions on how to participate in course learning activities.
4. The instructor clearly communicated important due dates/timeframes for learning activities.

Facilitation

5. The instructor was helpful in identifying areas of agreement and disagreement on course topics that helped me to learn.
6. The instructor was helpful in guiding the class towards understanding course topics in a way that helped me clarify my thinking.
7. The instructor helped to keep course participants engaged and participating in productive dialogue.
8. The instructor helped keep the course participants on task in a way that helped me to learn.
9. The instructor encouraged course participants to explore new concepts in this course.
10. Instructor actions reinforced the development of a sense of community among course participants.

Direct Instruction

11. The instructor helped to focus discussion on relevant issues in a way that helped me to learn.
12. The instructor provided feedback that helped me understand my strengths and weaknesses.
13. The instructor provided feedback in a timely fashion.

Social Presence

Interpersonal Relationships

14. Getting to know other course participants gave me a sense of belonging in the course.
15. I was able to form distinct impressions of some course participants.
16. Online or web-based communication is an excellent medium for social interaction.

Open Communication

17. I felt comfortable conversing through the online medium.
18. I felt comfortable participating in the course discussions.
19. I felt comfortable interacting with other course participants.

Group Cohesion

20. I felt comfortable disagreeing with other course participants while still maintaining a sense of trust.
21. I felt that my point of view was acknowledged by other course participants.
22. Online discussions help me to develop a sense of collaboration.

Cognitive Presence

Triggering Event

23. Problems posed increased my interest in course issues.
24. Course activities piqued my curiosity.
25. I felt motivated to explore content related questions.

Exploration

26. I utilized a variety of information sources to explore problems posed in this course.

27. Brainstorming and finding relevant information helped me resolve content-related questions.
28. Online discussions were valuable in helping me appreciate different perspectives.

Integration

29. Combining new information helped me answer questions raised in course activities.
30. Learning activities helped me construct explanations/solutions.
31. Reflection on course content and discussions helped me understand fundamental concepts in this class.

Resolution

32. I can describe ways to test and apply the knowledge created in this course.
33. I have developed solutions to course problems that can be applied in practice.
34. I can apply the knowledge created in this course to my work or other non-class related activities.

A Likert scale was used to measure the responses ranging from: 1 = strongly disagree, 2 = disagree, 3 = neutral, 4 = agree, 5 = strongly agree.

Further description and validation of this instrument can be found in:

Arbaugh, J. B., Cleveland-Innes, M., Diaz, S., Garrison, D. R., Ice, P., Richardson, J., Shea, P. and Swan, K. (2008) 'Developing a community of inquiry instrument: Testing a measure of the Community of Inquiry framework using a multi-institutional sample'. *Internet and Higher Education*, 11, pp. 133–136.

APPENDIX B

Shared Metacognition Survey Instrument

Self-regulation: When I am engaged in the learning process as an individual

SR1: I am aware of my effort.
SR2: I am aware of my thinking.
SR3: I know my level of motivation.
SR4: I question my thoughts.
SR5: I make judgments about the difficulty of a problem.
SR6: I am aware of my existing knowledge.
SR7: I am aware of my level of learning.
SR8: I assess my understanding.
SR9: I change my strategy when I need to.
SR10: I search for new strategies when needed.
SR11: I apply strategies.
SR12: I assess how I approach the problem.
SR13: I assess my strategies.

Co-regulation: When I am engaged in the learning process as a member of a group

CR1: I pay attention to the ideas of others.
CR2: I listen to the comments of others.
CR3: I consider the feedback of others.
CR4: I reflect upon the comments of others.

CR5: I observe the strategies of others.
CR6: I observe how others are doing.
CR7: I look for confirmation of my understanding from others.
CR8: I request information from others.
CR9: I respond to the contributions that others make.
CR10: I challenge the strategies of others.
CR11: I challenge the perspectives of others.
CR12: I help the learning of others.
CR13: I monitor the learning of others.

Items SR1 to SR7 were drafted to reflect monitoring strategies of self-regulation, while items SR8 to SR13 were drafted to reflect managing strategies of self-regulation. Similarly, items CR1 to CR6 and items CR7 to CR13 were drafted to reflect monitoring and managing strategies respectively. A Likert scale was used to measure the responses ranging from 1 indicating "very untrue of me" to 6 indicating "very true of me".

Further description and validation of this instrument can be found in:

Garrison, D. R. and Akyol, Z. (2015) 'Developing a shared metacognition construct and instrument: Conceptualizing and assessing metacognition in a community of inquiry'. *Internet and Higher Education*, 24, pp. 66–71.

REFERENCES

Abedin, B., Daneshgar, F. and D'Ambra, J. (2010) 'Underlying factors of sense of community in asynchronous computer supported collaborative learning environments'. *Journal of Online Learning and Teaching*, 6(3), pp. 585–597

Akyol, Z. and Garrison, D. R. (2008) 'The development of a community of inquiry over time in an online course: Understanding the progression and integration of social, cognitive and teaching presence'. *Journal of Asynchronous Learning Networks*, 12(3), pp. 3–22

Akyol, Z. and Garrison, D. R. (2011) 'Learning and satisfaction in online communities of inquiry' in S. B. Eom and J. B. Arbaugh (Eds) *Student Satisfaction and Learning Outcomes in e-learning: An Introduction to Empirical Research* (pp. 23–35). Hershey, PA: Information Science

Alavi, S. M. and Taghizadeh, M. (2013) 'Cognitive presence in virtual learning community: An EFL case'. *Journal of Distance Education*, 27(1). Retrieved December 4, 2014 from: www.ijede.ca/index.php/jde/article/view/818/1492

Allen, K. (2004) *An Interview with Dr. Kathleen Allen on Leading Collaboratively.* Retrieved September 29, 2014 from: file:///C:/Users/garrison/Downloads/Leading%20Collaborately%20Interview%20with%20Kathleen%20Allen.pdf

Amemado, D. J.-A. (2013) 'Pedagogical requirements in a university-context characterized by online and blended courses: Results from a study undertaken through fifteen Canadian universities' in Z. Akyol and D. R. Garrison (Eds) (2013) *Educational Communities of Inquiry: Theoretical Framework, Research and Practice* (pp. 401–427). Hershey, PA: IGI Global

Arbaugh, J. B. (2013) 'Does academic discipline moderate CoI-course outcomes relationships in online MBA courses?' *Internet and Higher Education*, 17, pp. 16–28

Arbaugh, J. B., Cleveland-Innes, M., Diaz, S., Garrison, D. R., Ice, P., Richardson, J., Shea, P. and Swan, K. (2008) 'Developing a community of inquiry instrument: Testing a measure of the Community of Inquiry framework using a multi-institutional sample'. *Internet and Higher Education*, 11, pp. 133–136

Argyris, C. (1976) 'Single loop and double loop models in research on decision making'. *Administrative Science Quarterly*, 21(3), pp. 363–375

Argyris, C. (1977) 'Organizational learning and management information systems accounting'. *Organizations and Society*, 2(2), pp. 113–123

Bai, H. (2009) 'Facilitating students' critical thinking in online discussion: An instructor's experience'. *Journal of Interactive Online Learning*, 8(2), pp. 156–164

Bierly, P. E., Stark, E. M. and Kessler, E. H. (2009) 'The moderating effects of virtuality on the antecedents and outcome of NPD team trust'. *Journal of Product Innovation Management*, 26, pp. 551–565

Boyer, E. L. (1990) *Scholarship Reconsidered: Priorities of the Professoriate.* Princeton, N.J: Carnegie Foundation for the Advancement of Teaching

Brown, J. S., Collins, A. and Duguid, P. (1989) 'Situated cognition and the culture of learning'. *Educational Researcher*, 18(1), pp. 32–42

Brynjolfsson, E. and McAfee, A. (2014) *The Second Machine Age: Work, Progress, and Prosperity in a Time of Brilliant Technologies.* NY: Norton

Buraphadeja, V. and Dawson, K. (2008) 'Content analysis in computer-mediated communication: Analyzing models for assessing critical thinking through the lens of social constructivism'. *American Journal of Distance Education*, 22(3), pp. 130–145

Caspi, A. and Blau, I. (2008) 'Social presence in online discussion groups: Testing three conceptions and their relations to perceived learning'. *Social Psychology of Education*, 11, pp. 323–346

Cecez-Kecmanovic, D. and Webb, C. (2000) 'Towards a communicative model of collaborative web-mediated learning'. *Australian Journal of Educational Technology*, 16(1), pp. 73–85

Chan, C. K. K. (2012) 'Co-regulation of learning in computer-supported collaborative learning environments: A discussion'. *Metacognition and Learning*, 7, pp. 63–73

Cho, M. and Kim, B. J. (2013) 'Students' self-regulation for interaction with others in online learning environments'. *Internet and Higher Education*, 17, pp. 69–75

Clarke, L. W. and Bartholomew, A. (2014) 'Digging beneath the surface: Analyzing the complexity of instructors' participation in asynchronous discussion'. *Journal of Asynchronous Learning Networks*, 18(3). Retrieved December 9, 2014 from: olj.onlinelearningconsortium.org/index.php/jaln/article/view/414/111

Cochrane, T. and Narayan, V. (2013) 'Redesigning professional development: Reconceptualising teaching using social learning technologies'. *Research in Learning Technology*, 21, pp. 1–19. Retrieved December 6, 2014 from: web.b.ebscohost.com.ezproxy.lib.ucalgary.ca/ehost/pdfviewer/pdfviewer?vid=3andsid=97d1a140-9308-4025-8421-035f25865bb9%40sessionmgr198andhid=109

Croxton, R. A. (2014) 'The role of interactivity in student satisfaction and persistence in online learning'. *Journal of Online Learning and Teaching*, 10(2), pp. 314–324

Cui, G., Lockee, B. and Meng, C. (2013) 'Building modern online social presence: A review of social presence theory and its instructional design implications for future trends'. *Education and Information Technologies*, 18(4), pp. 661–685

Dahlstrom, E. (2012) *ECAR Study of Undergraduate Students and Information Technology, 2012.* EDUCAUSE Center for Analysis and Research (ECAR). Retrieved November 8, 2014 from: net.educause.edu/ir/library/pdf/ERS1208/ERS1208.pdf

Dahlstrom, E. and Bichsel, J. (2014) *ECAR Study of Undergraduate Students and Information Technology, 2014.* EDUCAUSE Center for Analysis and Research (ECAR). Retrieved November 8, 2014 from: net.educause.edu/ir/library/pdf/ss14/ERS1406.pdf

Darabi, A., Arrastia, M. C., Nelson, D. W., Cornille, T. and Liang, X. (2011) 'Cognitive presence in asynchronous online learning: A comparison of four discussion strategies'. *Journal of Computer Assisted Learning*, 27, pp. 216–227

Daspit, J. J. and D'Souza, D. E. (2012) 'Using the community of inquiry framework to introduce Wiki environments in blended-learning pedagogies: Evidence from a business capstone course'. *Academy of Management Learning and Education*, 11(4), pp. 666–683

deNoyelles, A., Zydney, J. M. and Chen, B. (2014) 'Strategies for creating a community of inquiry through online asynchronous discussions'. *Journal of Online Learning and Teaching*, 10(1), pp. 153–165

Dewey, J. (1916) *Democracy and Education* (4th printing, 1964). New York: Macmillan

Dewey, J. (1933) *How We Think* (rev. ed.). Boston: D.C. Heath

Dewey, J. (1938) *Experience and Education* (7th printing, 1967). NY: Collier

Dewey, J. (1959) 'My pedagogic creed' in J. Dewey, *Dewey on education* (pp. 19–32). New York: Teachers College, Columbia University. (Original work published 1897)

DiDonato, N. C. (2013) 'Effective self- and co-regulation in collaborative learning groups: An analysis of how students regulate problem solving of authentic interdisciplinary tasks'. *Instructional Science*, 41, pp. 25–47

Dron, J. and Anderson, T. (2014) *The Distant Crowd: Transactional Distance and New Social Media Literacies.* Athabasca, Canada: AU Press

Duphorne, P. L. and Gunawardena, C. N. (2005) 'The effect of three computer conferencing designs on critical thinking skills of nursing students'. *The American Journal of Distance Education*, 19(1), pp. 37–50

Dyens, O. (2014) 'How artificial intelligence is about to disrupt higher education'. *University Affairs*. Retrieved April 30, 2014 from: www.university affairs.ca/how-artificial-intelligence-is-about-to-disrupt-higher-education.aspx

Engell, D., Woolley, A. W., Jing, L. X., Chabris, C. F. and Malone, T. W. (Dec 12, 2014) 'Reading the mind in the eyes or reading between the lines? Theory of mind predicts collective intelligence equally well online and face-to-face'. *PLoS ONE*, 9(12). Retrieved January 19, 2015 from: journals.plos.org/plosone/article?id=10.1371/journal.pone.0115212

Entwistle, N. J. and Ramsden, P. (1983) *Understanding Student Learning.* London: Croom Helm

Eom, S. B. and Arbaugh, J. B. (Eds) (2011) *Student Satisfaction and Learning Outcomes in e-learning: An Introduction to Empirical Research.* Hershey, PA: Information Science

Evans, T. D. and Haughey, M. (2014) 'Online distance education models and research implications' in O. Zawacki-Richter and T. Anderson (Eds) *Online Distance Education: Towards a Research Agenda* (pp. 131–149). Edmonton, Canada: Athabasca University Press

Evans, T. and Pauling, B. (2010) 'The future of distance education: Reformed, scrapped or recycled' in M. Cleveland-Innes and D. R. Garrison (Eds) (2010) *An Introduction to Distance Education: Understanding Teaching and Learning in a New Era* (pp. 198–223). London: Routledge

Featherman, S. (2014) *Higher Education at Risk: Strategies to Improve Outcomes, Reduce Tuition, and Stay Competitive in a Disruptive Environment.* Sterling, VA: Stylus Publishing

Feenberg, A. (1999) *Questioning Technology.* London: Routledge

Flavell, J. H. (1979) 'Metacognition and cognitive monitoring: A new area of cognitive–developmental inquiry'. *American Psychologist*, 34(10), pp. 906–911

Flavell, J. H. (1987) 'Speculations about the nature and development of metacognition' in F. Weinert and R. Kluwe (Eds) *Metacognition, Motivation and Understanding* (pp. 21–29). Hillsdale, NJ: Erlbaum

Garrison, D. R. (1987) 'Researching dropout in distance education: Some directional and methodological considerations'. *Distance Education*, 8(1), pp. 95–101

Garrison, D. R. (1989) *Understanding Distance Education: A Framework for the Future*. London: Routledge

Garrison, D. R. (1991) 'Critical thinking and adult education: A conceptual model for developing critical thinking in adult learners'. *International Journal of Lifelong Education*, 10(4), pp. 287–303

Garrison, D. R. (1997a) 'Self-directed learning: Toward a comprehensive model'. *Adult Education Quarterly*, 48(1), pp. 15–31

Garrison, D. R. (1997b) 'Computer conferencing: The post-industrial age of distance education'. *Open Learning*, 12(2), pp. 3–11

Garrison, D. R. (2000) 'Theoretical challenges for distance education in the 21st Century: A shift from structural to transactional issues'. *International Review of Research in Open and Distance Learning*, 1(1), pp. 1–17

Garrison, D. R. (2007) 'Online community of inquiry review: Social, cognitive and teaching presence issues'. *Journal of Asynchronous Learning Networks*, 11(1), pp. 61–72

Garrison, D. R. (2009) 'Communities of inquiry in online learning' in P. L. Rogers, G. A. Berg, J. V. Boettcher, C. Howard, L. Justice and K. D. Schenk (Eds) *Encyclopedia of Distance Learning* (2nd Ed.) (pp. 352–355). Hershey, PA: IGI Global

Garrison, D. R. (2011) *E-Learning in the 21st Century: A Framework for Research and Practice* (2nd Ed.). London: Routledge/Taylor and Francis

Garrison, D. R. (2013) 'Theoretical foundations and epistemological insights' in Z. Akyol and D. R. Garrison (Eds) *Educational Communities of Inquiry: Theoretical Framework, Research and Practice* (pp. 1–11). Hershey, PA: IGI Global

Garrison, D. R. and Akyol, Z. (2014) 'Developing a shared metacognition construct and instrument: Conceptualizing and assessing metacognition in a community of inquiry'. *Internet and Higher Education*, 24, pp. 66–71

Garrison, D. R. and Akyol, Z. (2015) 'Developing a shared metacognition construct and instrument: Conceptualizing and assessing metacognition in a community of inquiry'. *Internet and Higher Education*, 24, pp. 66–71

Garrison, D. R., Anderson, T. and Archer, W. (2001) 'Critical thinking, cognitive presence and computer conferencing in distance education'. *American Journal of Distance Education*, 15(1), pp. 7–23

Garrison, D. R., Anderson, T. and Archer, W. (2010) 'The first decade of the community of inquiry framework: A retrospective'. *Internet and Higher Education*, 13(1–2), pp. 5–9

Garrison, D. R. and Archer, W. (2000) *A Transactional Perspective on Teaching and Learning: A Framework for Adult and Higher Education*. Oxford, UK: Pergamon

Garrison, D. R. and Cleveland-Innes, M. (2005) 'Facilitating cognitive presence in online learning: Interaction is not enough'. *American Journal of Distance Education*, 19(3), pp. 133–148

Garrison, D. R., Cleveland-Innes, M. and Fung, T. S. (2010) 'Exploring causal relations among teaching, cognitive and social presence: A holistic view of the community of inquiry framework'. *Internet and Higher Education*, 13(1–2), pp. 31–36

Garrison, D. R. and Shale, D. (Eds) (1990) *Education at a Distance: From Issues to Practice*. Melbourne, FL: Krieger

Garrison, D. R. and Vaughan, N. (2008) *Blended Learning in Higher Education: Framework, Principles and Guidelines*. San Francisco: Jossey-Bass

Garrison, D. R. and Vaughan, N. D. (2013) 'Institutional change and leadership associated with blended learning innovation: Two case studies'. *Internet and Higher Education*, 18, pp. 24–28

Gasevic, D., Adesope, O., Joksimovic, S. and Kovanovic, V. (2015) 'Externally-facilitated regulation scaffolding and role assignment to develop cognitive presence in asynchronous online discussions'. *Internet and Higher Education*, 24, pp. 53–65

Ginsberg, B. (2011) *The Fall of the Faculty: The Rise of the All-administrative University and why it Matters*. Oxford: Oxford University Press

Gladwell, M. (2010) *Small Change*. Retrieved Oct 4, 2014 from *The New Yorker*. www.newyorker.com/reporting/2010/10/04/101004fa_fact_gladwell?currentPage=all

Goldstein, D. S., Leppa, C., Brockhaus, A., Bliquez, R. and Porter, I. (2013) 'Fostering social presence in a blended learning faculty development institute' in Z. Akyol, and D. R. Garrison, (Eds) (2013) *Educational Communities of Inquiry: Theoretical Framework, Research and Practice* (pp. 374–388). Hershey, PA: IGI Global

Gorsky, P., Caspi, A., Antonovsky, A., Blau, I. and Mansur, A. (2010) 'The relationship between academic discipline and dialogic behaviour in open university course forums'. *International Review of Research in Open and Distance Learning*, 11(2), pp. 49–72

Guri-Rosenblit, S. (2014) 'Distance education systems and institutions in the online era: An identity crisis' in O. Zawacki-Richter and T. Anderson

(Eds) *Online Distance Education: Towards a Research Agenda* (pp. 109–129). Edmonton, Canada: Athabasca University Press

Gutfreund, J. (2014) cited in White, C. C. R. *The End of Brick + Mortar? Not if Millennials Can Help It*. Retrieved January 13, 2015 from: www.ozy. com/fast-forward/the-end-of-brick-mortar-not-if-millennials-can-help-it/36448.article

Halverson, L. R., Graham, C. R., Spring, K. J., Drysdale, J. S. and Henrie, C. R. (2013) 'A thematic analysis of the most highly cited scholarship in the first decade of blended learning research'. *Internet and Higher Education*, 20, pp. 20–34

Hampton, K., Rainie, L., Lu, W., Dwyer, M., Shin, I. and Purcell, K. (2014) *Social Media and the 'Spiral of Silence'*. Retrieved September 8, 2014 from: www.pewinternet.org/2014/08/26/social-media-and-the-spiral-of-silence

Hart Research Associates (on behalf of The AAC&U) (2013) *It Takes More than a Major: Employer Priorities for College Learning and Student Success*. Washington, DC: Association of American Colleges and Universities (AAC&U) and Hart Research Associates. Retrieved December 13, 2014 from: www.aacu.org/leap/presidentstrust/compact/2013SurveySummary.cfm

He, W. (2013) 'Examining students' online interaction in a live video streaming environment using data and text mining'. *Computers in Human Behavior*, 29, pp. 90–102

Hemlin, S., Allwood, C. M. and Martin, B. R. (Eds) (2004) *Creative Knowledge Environments: The Influences on Creativity in Research*. UK: Edward Elgar Publishing

Holmberg, B. (1989) *Theory and Practice of Distance Education*. London: Routledge

Hunter, S. T. and Cushenbery, L. (2014) Is being a jerk necessary for originality? Examining the role of disagreeableness in the sharing and utilization of original ideas. *Journal of Business Psychology* (article not assigned to an issue) DOI: 10.1007/s10869-014-9386-1

Hutchins, E. (2000) 'Distributed cognition'. *International Encyclopedia of the Social and Behavioral Sciences*. Retrieved September 25, 2014 from: www. artmap-research.com/wp-content/uploads/2009/11/Hutchins_DistributedCognition.pdf

Ice, P. (2010) 'The future of learning technologies' in M. F. Cleveland-Innes and D. R. Garrison (Eds) *An Introduction to Distance Education: Understanding Teaching and Learning in a New Era* (pp. 137–164). London: Routledge

Ice, P., Gibson, A. M., Boston, W. and Becher, D. (2011) 'An exploration of differences between community of inquiry indicators in low and high disenrollment online courses'. *Journal of Asynchronous Learning Networks*, 15(2), pp. 44–69

Iiskala, T., Vauras, M., Lehtinen, E. and Salonen, P. (2011) 'Socially shared metacognition of dyads of pupils in collaborative mathematical problem-solving processes'. *Learning and Instruction*, 21, pp. 379–393

Ickenberry, S. (2001) 'Forward' in C. Latchem and D. Hanna (Eds) *Leadership for 21st Century Learning: Global Perspectives from Educational Perspectives*. Sterling, VA: Stylus Publishing

Isaacson, W. (2014) *The Innovators: How a Group of Hackers, Geniuses, and Geeks Created the Digital Revolution*. NY: Simon and Schuster

Jackson, L. C., Jackson, A. C. and Chambers, D. (2013) 'Establishing an online community of inquiry at the Distance Education Centre, Victoria'. *Distance Education*, 34(3), pp. 353–367

Jafarian, S. (unpublished) 'Learner's critical thinking disposition in blended learning environment: The influence of community of inquiry'. Submitted to the *British Journal of Educational Technology*

Janssen, J., Erkens, G. and Kirschner, P. A. (2012) 'Task-related and social regulation during online collaborative learning'. *Metacognition Learning*, 7(1), pp. 25–43

Jo, Y. J., Lim, K. Y. and Kim, E. K. (2011) 'Online university students' satisfaction and persistence: Examining perceived level of presence, usefulness and ease of use as predictors in a structural model'. *Computers and Education*, 57(2), pp. 1654–1664

Johnson, D. W. and Johnson, R. T. (2009) 'An educational psychology success story: Social interdependence theory and cooperative learning'. *Educational Researcher*, 38(5), pp. 365–379

Jones, C., Dirckinck-Holmfeld, L. and Lindstrom, B. (2006) 'A relational, indirect, meso-level approach to CSCL design in the next decade'. *Computer Supported Collaborative Learning*, 1(1), pp. 35–56

Jones, S. J. and Meyer, K. A. (2012) 'Introduction to the special issue: Faculty development for online teaching'. *Journal of Asynchronous Learning Networks*, 16(2), pp. 5–7

Kennedy, D. and Kennedy, N. S. (2013) 'Community of philosophical inquiry online and off: Retrospectus and prospectus' in Z. Akyol and D. R. Garrison (Eds) *Educational Communities of Inquiry: Theoretical Framework, Research and Practice* (pp. 12–29). Hershey, PA: IGI Global

Kennedy, N. and Kennedy, D. (2010) 'Between chaos and entropy: Community of inquiry from a systems perspective'. *Complicity: An*

International Journal of Complexity and Education, 7, 2. ejournals.library. ualberta.ca/index.php/complicity/index

Kennedy, G. E., Judd, T. S., Churchward, A., Gray, K. and Krause, K. (2008) 'First year students' experiences with technology: Are they really digital natives?' *Australasian Journal of Educational Technology*, 24(1), pp. 108–122

Kenny, R. W. (1998) *Reinventing Undergraduate Education: A Blueprint for America's Research Universities.* Stony Brook, NY: University of New York

Kim, Y. R., Park, M. S., Moore, T. J. and Varma, S. (2013) 'Multiple levels of metacognition and their elicitation through complex problem-solving tasks'. *Journal of Mathematical Behavior*, 32(3), pp. 377–396

King, P. M. and Kitchener, K. S. (1994) *Developing Reflective Judgment.* San Francisco: Jossey-Bass

Kirschner, P. A. and van Merrienboer, J. J. G. (2013) 'Do learners really know best? Urban legends in education'. *Educational Psychologist*, 48(3), pp. 169–183

Kovanovic, V., Joksimovic, S., Gasevic, D. and Hatala, M. (2014) 'What is the source of social capital? The association between social network position and social presence in communities of inquiry' in S. Gutiérrez-Santos and O. C. Santos (2014) *The Graph-based Educational Data Mining Workshop in Extended Proceedings 2014 Educational Data Mining Conference.* London, UK: CEUR-WS. Retrieved from: kovanovic.info/wp-content/uploads/2014/11/Kovanovic-et-al.-2014-What-is-the-source-of-social-capital-The-associat.pdf

Kozan, K. and Richardson, J. C. (2014) 'Interrelationships between and among social, teaching, and cognitive presence'. *Internet and Higher Education.* 21, pp. 68–73

Kuh, G. D. (2009) 'The National Survey of Student Engagement: Conceptual and Empirical Foundations'. *New Directions for Institutional Research.* 141, pp. 5–20

Kuh, G. D. (2000) *The National Survey of Student Engagement: The College Student Report.* Bloomington: Indiana University Center for Postsecondary Research and Planning

Kuhn, T. S. (1962) *The Structure of Scientific Revolutions.* Chicago: University of Chicago Press

Kumar, S., Dawson, K., Black, E. W., Cavanaugh, C. and Sessums, C. D. (2011) 'Applying the Community of Inquiry framework to an online professional practice doctoral program'. *The International Review of Research in Open and Distance Learning*, 12(6), pp. 126–142. Retrieved from: web.a.ebscohost.com.ezproxy.lib.ucalgary.ca/ehost/pdfviewer/pdfviewer?vid=2andsid=dd38c4a1-71f2-4ac1-8637-3634381e9242%40sessionmgr4005andhid=4214

Kupczynski, L., Ice, P., Wiesenmeyer, R. and McCluskey, F. (2010) 'Student perceptions of the relationship between indicators of teaching presence and success in online courses'. *Journal of Interactive Online Learning*, 9(1), pp. 23–43

Lambert, J. L. and Fisher, J. L. (2013) 'Community of inquiry framework: Establishing community in an online course'. *Journal of Interactive Online Learning*, 12(1), pp. 1–16

Larkin, S. (2009) 'Socially mediated metacognition and learning to write'. *Thinking Skills and Creativity*, 4(3), pp. 149–159

Lee, C. D. and Smagorinsky, P. (2000) 'Introduction: Constructing meaning through collaboration' in C. C. Lee and P. Smagorinsky (Eds) *Vygotskian Perspectives on Literacy Research: Constructing Meaning through Collaborative Inquiry* (pp. 1–15). Cambridge, UK: Cambridge University Press

Lee, S. M. (2014) 'The relationships between higher order thinking skills, cognitive density, and social presence in online learning'. *Internet and Higher Education*, 21, pp. 41–51

Leng, B.A., Dolmans, D. H., Jobsis, R., Muijtjens, A. M. and Van Der Vleuten, C. P. (2009) 'Exploration of an e-learning model to foster critical thinking on basic science concepts during work placements'. *Computers and Education*, 53(1), pp. 1–13

Leong, P. (2011) 'Role of social presence and cognitive absorption in online learning environments'. *Distance Education*, 32(1), pp. 5–28

Lewin, K. (1945) 'The research center for group dynamics at the Massachusetts Institute of Technology'. *Sociometry*, 8, pp. 125–135

Lewin, T. (2013, April 30) 'Colleges adapt online courses to ease burden'. *New York Times*, p. A1

Lin, X., Hu, X., Hu, Q. and Liu, Z. (2014) 'A social network analysis of teaching and research collaboration in a teachers' virtual learning community'. *British Journal of Educational Technology* DOI: 10.1111/bjet.12234

Lipman, M. (2003) *Thinking in Education* (2nd Ed.). Cambridge, UK: Cambridge University Press

Liyanagunawardena, T. R., Adams, A. A. and Williams, S. A. (2013) 'MOOCs: A systematic study of the published literature 2008–2012'. *The International Review of Research in Open and Distance Learning*, 14(3), pp. 202–227

Ma, J., Han, X., Yang, J. and Cheng, J. (2015) 'Examining the necessary condition for engagement in an online learning environment based on learning analytics approach: The role of the instructor'. *Internet and Higher Education*, 24, pp. 26–34

MacKnight, C. B. (2000) 'Teaching critical thinking through online discussions'. *Educause Quarterly*, 4, pp. 38–41

Martinez-Aleman, A. M. (2012) *Accountability, Pragmatic Aims and the American University*. New York, NY: Routledge

Marton, F. and Saljo, R. (1976) 'On qualitative differences in learning: 1 – outcome and process'. *British Journal of Educational Psychology*, 46, pp. 4–11

Massoni, S. (2014) 'Emotion as a boost to metacognition: How worry enhances the quality of confidence'. *Consciousness and Cognition*, 29, pp. 189–198

Matthews, D., Bogle, L., Boles, E., Day, S. and Swan, K. (2013) 'Developing communities of inquiry in online courses: A design-based approach' in Z. Akyol and D. R. Garrison (Eds) (2013) *Educational Communities of Inquiry: Theoretical Framework, Research and Practice* (pp. 490–508). Hershey, PA: IGI Global

McPeck, J. E. (1990) *Teaching Critical Thinking*. New York, NY: Routledge, Chapman and Hall

Means, B., Toyama, Y., Murphy, R., Bakia, M. and Jones, K. (2009) *Evaluation of Evidence-Based Practices in Online Learning: A Meta-Analysis and Review of Online Learning Studies*. Washington, DC: US Department of Education, Office of Planning, Evaluation, and Policy Development. Retrieved November 19, 2014 from: www.ed.gov/rschstat/eval/tech/evidence-based-practices/finalreport.pdf

Moore, J. C. and Shelton, K. (2013) 'Social and student engagement and support: The Sloan-C Quality Scorecard for the Administration of Online Programs'. *Journal of Asynchronous Learning Networks*, 17(1) pp. 53–72

Nickerson, R. S. (1998) 'Confirmation bias: A ubiquitous phenomenon in many guises'. *Review of General Psychology*, 2(2) pp. 175–220

NMC Horizon Report (2014) New Media Consortium, Austin, Texas. Retrieved from: www.nmc.org/pdf/2014-nmc-horizon-report-he-EN.pdf

Online Learning News (2015, January 2014) 'Are massive open online courses (MOOCs) enabling a new pedagogy? Contact North'. Retrieved January 14, 2015 from: contactnorth.ca/trends-directions/are-massive-open-online-courses-moocs-enabling-new-pedagogy

Paulus, P. B., Nijstad, B. A. and Nijstad, B. A. (Eds) (2003) *Group Creativity: Innovation through Collaboration*. New York, NY: Oxford University Press

Peters, O. (1994a) 'Distance education and industrial production: A comparative interpretation in outline (1973)' in Keegan, D. (Ed.) *Otto Peters on Distance Education: The Industrialization of Teaching and Learning* (pp. 107–127). London: Routledge

Peters, O. (1994b) 'Introduction' in Keegan, D. (Ed.) *Otto Peters on Distance Education: The Industrialization of Teaching and Learning* (pp. 1–23). London: Routledge

Pike, G. R., Kuh, G. D. and McCormick, A. C. (2011) 'An investigation of the contingent relationships between learning community participation and student engagement'. *Research in Higher Education*, 52, pp. 300–322

Pinto, D. (2014) 'The chair of 2014: Faculty, administrator, and academic leader'. *The Department Chair*, 25(1)

Porter, W. W., Graham, C. R., Spring, K. A. and Welch, K. R. (2014) 'Blended learning in higher education: Institutional adoption and implementation'. *Computers and Education*, 75, pp. 185–195

Prawat, R. S. (1992) 'Teachers' beliefs about teaching and learning. A constructivist perspective'. *American Journal of Education*, 100(3), pp. 354–395

Prichett, C. C., Wohleb, E. C. and Pritchett, C. G. (2013) 'Educators' perceived importance of Web 2.0 technology applications'. *TechTrends*, 57(2), pp. 33–38

Purzer, S. (2011) 'The relationship between team discourse, self-efficacy, and individual achievement: A sequential mixed-methods study'. *Journal of Engineering Education*, 100(4), pp. 655–679

Raffaghelli, J. E., Ghislandi, P. and Yang, N. (2014) 'Quality as perceived by learners: Is it the dark side of the MOOCs?' *Research on Education and Media*, VI(1), pp. 121–136

Rodriguez, C. O. (2012) 'MOOCs and the AI-Stanford like courses: Two successful and distinct course formats for massive open online courses'. *European Journal of Open, Distance and E-Learning*, 2. Retrieved November 10, 2014 from: www.eurodl.org/materials/contrib/2012/Rodriguez.pdf

Rodriguez, B. C. P. and Armellini, A. (2014) 'Applying the interaction equivalency theorem to online courses in a large organization'. *Journal of Interactive Online Learning*, 13(2), pp. 51–66

Rogers, P. and Lea, M. (2005) 'Social presence in distributed group environments: The role of social identity'. *Behavior & Information Technology*, 24(2), pp. 151–158

Rohman, J. (2014a) *Great Place to Work: Guide to Greatness.* Retrieved September 1, 2014 from: createyours.greatplacetowork.com/rs/greatplacetowork/images/Great_Place_to_Work_Guide_to_Greatness_download.pdf?mkt_tok=3RkMMJWWfF9wsRoisq3AZKXonjHpfsX8 7%2BwrW6W%2FlMI%2F0ER3fOvrPUfGjI4FSsJnI%2BSLDwEYGJl v6SgFQrnAMbduzrgMXhM%3D

Rohman, J. (2014b) *5 Lessons for Leaders as They Build a Great Workplace.* Retrieved September 1, 2014 from: createyours.greatplacetowork.com/rs/greatplacetowork/images/2014-5-Lessons-for-Leaders-whitepaper-fnl.pdf?utm_source=marketoandutm_medium=emailandutm_content=whitepaper-pdf-downloadandutm_campaign=5-lessons-for-leadersandmkt_tok=3RkMMJWWfF9wsRojvqTJZKXonjHpfsX87%2

BwrW6W%2FlMI%2F0ER3fOvrPUfGjI4ESMJgI%2BSLDwEYGJlv6
SgFQrnAMbduzrgMXhM%3D

Rourke, L., Anderson, T., Garrison, D. R. and Archer, W. (2001) 'Assessing social presence in asynchronous, text-based computer conferencing'. *Journal of Distance Education*, 14(3), pp. 51–70

Rowntree, D. (1977) *Assessing Students*. London: Harper and Row

Rubin, B. and Fernandes, R. (2013) 'Measuring the community in online classes'. *Journal of Asynchronous Learning Networks*, 17(3), pp. 115–130

Saade, R. G., Morin, D. and Thomas, J. D. E. (2012) 'Critical thinking in e-learning environments'. *Computers in Human Behavior*, 28, pp. 1608–1617

Saritas, T. (2008) 'The construction of knowledge through social interaction via computer-mediated communication'. *The Quarterly Review of Distance Education*, 9(1), pp. 35–49

Sawyer, R. K. (Ed.) (2006) *The Cambridge Handbook of the Learning Sciences*. Cambridge, UK: Cambridge University Press

Sawyer, R. K. (2008) 'Optimising learning: Implications of learning sciences research' Chapter 2 in *Innovating to Learn: Learning to Innovate* (2008). OECD

Schleicher, A. (2010) *Skills Beyond School*. OCED. Retrieved from: www.oecd.org/edu/skills-beyond-school/andreasschleicher-deputydirectorforeducationandspecialadvisoroneducationpolicytotheoecdssecretary-general.htm

Schrage, M. (1995) *No More Teams: Mastering the Dynamics of Creative Collaboration*. New York, NY: Currency Doubleday

Schraw, G. (2001) 'Promoting general metacognitive awareness' in H. J. Hartman (Ed.) *Metacognition in Learning and Instruction: Theory, Research and Practice* (pp. 3–16). Boston: Kluwer

Semingson, P. and White, K. (2012) 'Developing pre-service teachers' knowledge about phonics via video-based modules and discussion prompts' in P. Resta (Ed.) *Proceedings of Society for Information Technology and Teacher Education International Conference 2012* (pp. 2092–2097). Chesapeake, VA: AACE

Shea, P. and Bidjerano, T. (2009) 'Cognitive presence and online learner engagement: A cluster analysis of the community of inquiry framework'. *Journal of Computing in Higher Education*, 21, pp. 199–217

Shea, P., Hayes, S., Uzuner-Smith, S., Gozza-Cohen, M., Vickers, J. and Bidjerano, T. (2014) 'Reconceptualizing the community of inquiry framework: Exploratory and confirmatory analysis'. *Internet and Higher Education*, 23, pp. 9–17

Shea, P., Vickers, J. and Hayes, S. (2010) 'Online instructional effort measured through the lens of teaching presence in the Community of Inquiry framework: A re-examination of measures and approach'. *International Review of Research in Open and Distance Learning*, 11(3). Retrieved December 6, 2014 from: web.b.ebscohost.com.ezproxy.lib.ucalgary.ca/ehost/pdfviewer/pdfviewer?vid=2andsid=364c1d80-6b7d-47ae-9ae2-62fb2488ccd4%40sessionmgr112andhid=118

Sheridan, K. and Kelly, M. A. (2010) 'The indicators of instructor presence that are important to students in online courses'. *Journal of Online Learning and Teaching*, 6(4), pp. 767–778

Sherratt, C. (2012) 'Synergy, supervision and self-reliance: Perceptions of the role of the tutor in a postgraduate online learning programme'. *E–Learning and Digital Media*, 9(1), pp. 100–112

Short, J., Williams, E. and Christie, B. (1976) *The Social Psychology of Telecommunications*. London: Wiley

Simonson, M., Schlosser, C. and Orellana, A. (2011) 'Distance education research: A review of the literature'. *Journal of Computing in Higher Education*, (23), pp. 124–42

Sins, P. H. M., Savelsbergh, E. R., van Joolingen, W. R. and van Hout-Wolters, B. H. A. M. (2011) 'Effects of face-to-face versus chat communication on performance in a collaborative inquiry modeling task'. *Computers and Education*, 56, pp. 379–387

Snyder, M. M. and Dringus, L.P. (2014) 'An exploration of metacognition in asynchronous student-led discussions: A qualitative inquiry'. *Journal of Asynchronous Learning Networks*, 18(2), pp. 29–48

So, H.-J. and Brush, T. A. (2008) 'Student perceptions of collaborative learning, social presence and satisfaction in a blended learning environment: Relationships and crucial factors'. *Computers and Education*, 51, pp. 318–336

Son, L. K., Kornell, N., Finn, B. and Cantlon, J. F. (2012) 'Metacognition and the social animal' in P. Brinol and K. G. Demarree (Eds) *Social Metacognition* (pp. 159–177). NY: Taylor and Francis

Stein, D. S., Wanstreet, C. E., Slagle, P., Trinko, L. A. and Lutz, M. (2013) 'From 'hello' to higher-order thinking: The effect of coaching and feedback on online chats'. *Internet and Higher Education*, 16, pp. 78–84

Sternberg, R. J. (2013) 'Giving employers what they don't really want'. *The Chronicle of Higher Education*, June 17. Retrieved August 15, 2014 from: chronicle.com/article/Giving-Employers-What-They/139877/?cid=ja

Swan, K., Day, S. L., Bogle, L. R. and Matthews, D. B. (2014) 'A collaborative, design-based approach to improving an online program'. *Internet and Higher Education*, 21, pp. 74–81

Szeto, E. (2015) 'Community of Inquiry as an instructional approach: What effects of teaching, social and cognitive presences are there in blended synchronous learning and teaching?' *Computers and Education*, 81, pp. 191–201

The Chronicle of Higher Education and American Public Media's *Marketplace* (December, 2012) *The Role of Higher Education in Career Development: Employer Perceptions*. Retrieved from: chronicle.com/items/biz/pdf/Employers%20Survey.pdf

Thompson, C. (2013) *Smarter than You Think: How Technology is Changing our Minds for the Better*. New York: Penguin Press

Toven-Lindsey, B., Rhoads, R. A. and Lozano, J. B. (2015) 'Virtually unlimited classrooms: Pedagogical practices in massive open online courses'. *Internet and Higher Education*, 24, pp. 1–12

Vaughan, N. D., Cleveland-Innes, M. and Garrison, D. R. (2013) *Teaching in Blended Learning Environments: Creating and Sustaining Communities of Inquiry*. Edmonton, Canada: Athabasca University Press

Vaughan, N. and Garrison, D. R. (2006) 'How blended learning can support a faculty development community of inquiry'. *Journal of Asynchronous Learning Networks*, 10(4), pp. 139–152

Vygotsky, L. S. (1978) *Mind in Society: The Development of Higher Psychological Processes*. Cambridge, MA: Harvard University Press

Wade, S. E. and Fauske, J. R. (2004) 'Dialogue online: Prospective teachers' discourse strategies in computer-mediated discussions'. *Reading Research Quarterly*, 39(2), pp. 134–160

Wasson, C. (2013) '"It was like a little community": An ethnographic study of online learning and its implications for MOOCs'. *Ethnographic Praxis in Industry Conference Proceedings*. Retrieved November 10, 2014 from: onlinelibrary.wiley.com/doi/10.1111/j.1559-8918.2013.00017.x/pdf

Weerasinghe, T. A., Ramberg, R. and Hewagamage, K. P. (2012) 'Inquiry-based learning with or without facilitator interactions'. *Journal of Distance Education*, 26(2). Retrieved from: www.jofde.ca/index.php/jde/article/view/779/1406

Wells, G. (2000) 'Dialogic inquiry in education: Building on the legacy of Vygotsky' in C. D. Lee and P. Smagorinsky (Eds) *Vygotskian Perspectives on Literacy Research: Constructing Meaning through Collaborative Inquiry* (pp. 51–85). New York, NY: Cambridge University Press

White, B. Y., Frederiksen, J. R. and Collins, A. (2009) 'The interplay of scientific inquiry and metacognition: More than a marriage of convenience' in D. Hacker, J. Dunlosky and A. Graesser (Eds) *Handbook of Metacognition in Education* (pp. 175–205). New York: Routledge

White, C. C. R. (2014) 'The End of Brick + Mortar? Not if Millennials Can Help It'. Retrieved January 15, 2015 from: www.ozy.com/ fast-forward/the-end-of-brick-mortar-not-if-millennials-can-help-it/36448.article

Wilson, E. O. (2012) *The Social Conquest of Earth*. New York, NY: W.W. Norton

Wisneski, J. E., Ozogul, G. and Bichelmeyer, B. A. (2015) 'Does teaching presence transfer between MBA teaching environments? A comparative investigation of instructional design practices associated with teaching presence'. *Internet and Higher Education*, 25, pp. 18–27

Woodley, A. and Simpson, O. (2014) 'Student dropout: The elephant in the room' in O. Zawacki-Richter and T. Anderson (Eds) *Online Distance Education: Towards a Research Agenda* (pp. 459–483). Edmonton, Canada: Athabasca University Press

Woolley, A., Malone, T. W. and Chabris, W. (2015) 'Why some teams are smarter than others'. *The New York Times* (Jan 15). Retrieved January 19, 2015 from: www.nytimes.com/2015/01/18/opinion/sunday/why-some-teams-are-smarter-than-others.html?_r=0

Zawacki-Richter, O. and Anderson, T. (2014) 'Introduction: Research areas in online distance education' in O. Zawacki-Richter and T. Anderson (Eds) (2014) *Online Distance Education: Towards a Research Agenda* (pp. 1–35). Edmonton, Canada: AU Press

Zhan, Z. and Mei, H. (2013) 'Academic self-concept and social presence in face-to-face and online learning: Perceptions and effects on students' learning achievement and satisfaction across environments'. *Computers and Education*, 69, pp. 131–138

Zhao, H., Sullivan, K. P. H. and Mellenius, I. (2014) 'Participation, interaction and social presence: An exploratory study of collaboration in online peer review groups'. *British Journal of Educational Technology*, 45(5), pp. 807–819

Zydney, J. M., deNoyelles, A. and Seo, K. K. (2012) 'Creating a community of inquiry in online environments: An exploratory study on the effect of a protocol on interactions within asynchronous discussions'. *Computers and Education*, 58, pp. 77–87

INDEX

Page numbers in italic refer to tables or figures.